Guide for Beginners

Mastering

Adobe

EXPRESS

24

Ebenezer Hrehaan

Copyright 2024 © Ebenezer Hrehaan

All rights reserved. This book is copyright and no part of it may be reproduced, stored or transmitted, in any form or means, without the prior written permission of the copyright owner.

Printed in the United States of America

Copyright 2024 © Ebenezer Hrehaan.

CONTENTS

INTRODUCTION 1
   Overview of Adobe Express 1
      Get to know about our community 2
      Uncover all of Adobe Express incredible features. 2
      Cost of an Adobe Express membership 5
      Adobe Express for Teams, Enterprise, and Education 6
      Getting the Adobe Express 6
   Adobe Express System Requirements 7
      Adobe Express on the web 7
      Technical requirements 8
      Quick action image requirements 8
   Language versions available 9
   Keyboard Shortcuts 9
      Common Actions 10
      Move, Rotate & Arrange 10
      Selection 11
      Grouping 11
      Zoom 12
      Edit video 13
      Edit text 14
   Progressive Web Application 15
      Installing the Progressive Web Application 15
      Benefits of the Progressive Web Apps (PWA) 15
   Installing your Adobe Express PWAs 16
   Effortlessly accessing your Adobe Express Progressive Web App 16

ADDING THE ADOBE EXPRESS BROWSER EXTENSION 17

    Installing your Adobe Express Chrome extension 17

    Pining your extension on your browser toolbar 17

    Launching your Adobe Express extension 18

        Editing your image 18

        Using your images quick actions 18

    Most commonly asked questions 19

    When I attempt to open the extension, I receive an error message. What should I do after that? 19

    How will I save image that is edited on Adobe's Express web files? 20

    If I don't type a URL into my address bar, will my pinned view still work? 20

    When I try to modify an image or do a quick action, why am I receiving an error warning (Unknown error)? 20

    When I attempt to use my Adobe Express's extension with my Enterprise account, a blocked screen appears. How do I open the extension on my end? 21

MOBILE APP 22

    Adobe Express mobile beta overview 22

    Scaning the QR code to get started on mobile 23

    Verify your eligibility & get started 24

GENERATE AND EDIT GRAPHICS, VIDEOS and PHOTOS 26

    Working with Adobe Illustrator and Photoshop creative assets 26

    Adding Linked Asset 26

    Editing Linked Asset 27

    Importing your file 28

IMPORTING AND ENHANCING PDFS WITHIN ADOBE EXPRESS 29

    Importing PDF file to your Adobe Express 29

    Enhance PDF files 30

Adding or replacing images 30

Add or edit text 30

Adding assets, logos, & more 30

Adding pages 31

GETTING STARTED WITH THE ADOBE EXPRESS TEMPLATES 32

Getting started with template 32

What comes next? 33

CREATING NEW TEMPLATE FROM SCRATCH 34

Create a fresh template from starting. 34

What comes next? 35

CREATING WEBPAGE WITH ADOBE EXPRESS 36

Creating your webpage 36

Adding various visual assets on your webpage 38

Adding custom themes to a webpage 39

ADDING MULTIPLE PAGES TO ADOBE EXPRESS FILES 40

Getting started with the multiple pages 40

What comes next? 41

CREATE VIDEO WITH ADOBE EXPRESS 42

Getting started with video 42

Adding scenes into your timeline 43

Adjust timing of any layer in your video 43

Locate your timed objects in any scene 43

Adjusting timing of your audio track 44

FINDING AND SUBMITING ADOBE STOCK CONTENT ID 46

ANIMATE PHOTOS, TEXT, AND VIDEOS ON ADOBE EXPRESS 48

Animate text, photos and videos 48

In 49

Out 49

Looping 50

What comes next? 51

IMPORTING COLOUR THEMES INTO ADOBE EXPRESS.............................. 52

TRANSLATE YOUR FILES AND YOUR TEMPLATES.. 54

Translate content.. 54

Commonly asked questions 55

How is the Translate feature implemented?.. 55

The language in my file differs from the detected source language. How should I proceed? 55

What languages can I translate to? 55

Is there any limit on the amount of languages I am able to translate into at once? 56

When translating, does one have a maximum number of character limit? 56

Will the translation affect the font used in my text? 56

WORKING WITH LAYERS 57

Learn layer basics... 57

Open the layer pane 57

Rearrange layers 57

Group & ungroup objects in designs 58

Lock layers.. 58

USING CHATGPT TO EXPLORE THE ADOBE EXPRESS TEMPLATES 59

Explore templates... 59

Chatting with the Adobe Express GPT 60

PRESENTATION 61

Importing PowerPoint file.. 61

Result 61

Explore presentation templates 62

Result 62

Manage pages.. 63

Presenting your design 64

Result 64

BACKGROUNDS 66

Adding background image on your design 66

Removing background from your video 66

Replacing page backgrounds from images 67

GENERATIVE AI 69

Generating images from text with generative AI 69

Generate extraordinary images for your designs using Text to image 69

Generating text effects with generative AI... 71

Using text effects to add impact to your designs. 71

What comes next? 73

Inserting or replacing objects using your Generative fill............................ 73

Insert or replace objects 73

Removing objects from your image with the Generative fill..................... 74

Removing objects from your image... 75

Generate editable templates using Text to Template 76

Create customizable templates 76

Tips to make your ideas come to life 76

CREATING AND MANAGING BRANDS 78

Creating brand in Adobe Express... 78

Creating your brand 78

What comes next? 79

Managing shared brands in Express 79
    Share a brand 79
    Getting started to access the shared brands 80
    Leaving shared brand with you 80

ADDING CUSTOM FONTS 81

Adding customs fonts to your Brand on Adobe Express 81

Adding your custom fonts into your file on Adobe Express 82

Supported font files 82

Commonly asked questions 83

    After my express membership expires, what will happen to the fonts? 83

    If my brand is deleted, what will happen to the fonts? 83

    I get a message saying that my brand-named file is locked when I attempt to open it. HOW can I Access MY FILE? 83

    How do I use a shared brand with a restricted font? 84

    If I have an education account, how can i access the custom fonts? 84

    Is it possible for me to coedit a file with a font that another user uploaded? 85

CREATING AND SHARING CREATIVE CLOUD LIBRARIES 86

    Create Libraries 86

    Share Libraries 87

    Accepting invite to Libraries 87

    What comes next? 87

LOCKING AND UNLOCKING ELEMENTS IN YOUR DESIGNS 88

    Lock & unlock your text 88

    Locking and unlocking images 88

    What comes next? 89

SET BRAND STYLE CONTROLS ON TEMPLATES 90

Style restrictions 90

Sharing template with controlled permissions... 91

What comes next? 92

Create from shared template 92

CONTENT SCHEDULER 94

Overview of Content Scheduler.. 94

For Content Scheduler to work, which subscription is required? 95

What is the function of Content Scheduler? 95

.... 96

Connecting your social accounts 96

  Connecting your social accounts to your Content Scheduler................ 97

  Connect Facebook 97

Connecting your Instagram through Facebook account 98

  Connect Pinterest, X (Twitter), LinkedIn, / TikTok.................................. 99

  Commonly Asked Queries.. 99

Schedule and publish social media posts 102

  Scheduling and publishing social media posts................................... 102

Media specifications of your social media posts 103

  Facebook.. 103

  Instagram 104

  X (Twitter) 105

  LinkedIn.. 106

  Pinterest... 106

  TikTok... 107

QUICK ACTION 108

Resizing images with Quick Actions... 108

  Resize your image to make spectacular designs................................ 108

What comes next? 109

Removing background from your image with Quick Action 109

    Effortlessly remove your image background in one click 109

    What comes next? 110

Converting the file formats of your images with the Quick Actions 111

    Convert images 111

    Supported file formats 112

    What comes next? 112

Cropping your image with the Quick Action 112

    Effortlessly crop your images within seconds 113

Animate your character using audio 113

    Animating characters from audios and incorporate it into your designs 114

Adding captions on videos with the Quick actions 115

    Adding captions 116

Trim your videos with Quick Action 117

    Trim video to it best length 117

    What comes next? 117

Resizing your video with Quick Actions 118

    Resizing video for every social media platforms 118

Converting video to GIF with Quick Actions 119

    Transforming your videos to appealing GIFs 120

    Converting videos into MP4 with Quick Actions 120

    Transforming videos to MP4 120

Crop videos within seconds with Quick Actions 121

    Cropping a video 121

Merging images and videos with Quick Actions 122

Merging your Images and videos easily within Adobe Express 122

Converting from or to PDF with Quick Actions 123
    Converting PDFs 123
    What comes next? 123

Editing your PDF images and text with Quick Action 124
    Editing PDF images and text on Adobe Express 124

Combining files into single PDF with Quick Actions 125
    Combine files 125
    What comes next? 126

Organizing your Pages into single PDF with Quick Actions 126
    Organize Pages to single PDF 127
    What comes next? 128

Generating QR code with Quick Actions 128
    Generating QR codes and using it to customize your designs in Adobe Express 129
    Generate a QR code 129
    Using your QR code for designing menu within Adobe Express 130
    What comes next? 130

PUBLISH AND SHARE 131

Collaborate and comment in Adobe Express 131
    Inviting Collaborators to share your files 131
    Place a pin to give context to your comment 132
    Tag and notify others of your comments 132
    What comes next? 133

Host webpage with Adobe Express 133
    Host webpage using unique URL 133
    Commonly asked questions 134

- What's web hosting? 134
  - What does Adobe Express web hosting entail? 134
  - Can I use a different server to host content? 134
  - What is the present maximum number of hosted published Express creations, if any? 135
- Copying files between your accounts 135
  - Copying files among accounts 135
- Privacy and permissions 137
  - What will happen and who can view a link that I share? 137
  - How can I unpublish a previous shared file from publication? 137

ADOBE EXPRESS ON MOBILE 139

- Adobe Express for iOS 139
- Sign in 139
- Getting started with the Adobe Express 140
- Creating designs & collages 140
- Viewing and managing your projects 144
- Deleting your projects in mass 146
- Sync projects across your platforms 146

DISABLING OF REMIXABLE LINKS IN THE EXPRESS FAQ 148

- What's remixable link? 148
- When the shareable template remixable links are disabled, what should I expect? 148
- My files are not accessible to the person with whom I shared my remixable link. How can I allow them to access? 148
- I've shared links to remixable content on public platforms like marketplaces and websites. Now that the remixable links are disabled, what should I do? 149
- Can I still access my files? 149

When Adobe Express is updated, will the remixable link capabilities be restored?..149

Adobe Express for Android 150

    Sign in..150

    Getting started with Adobe Express...150

    Getting to know your workspace..151

    Create designs and collages...152

Your Projects...158

Managing Express subscriptions in iOS...160

    Downloading and installing Adobe Express on iOS 160

    Cancelling your Express subscription...160

Manage Express subscriptions in Android..161

    Download & install Adobe Express in Android 161

    Cancellation & refund...161

Manage Adobe Express subscriptions on Samsung Galaxy Store 162

    Download and install Adobe Express for Samsung from the Galaxy Store 162

    Upgrading into paid Express for subscription of Samsung 162

    Cancel your Express subscription 163

INTRODUCTION

Overview of Adobe Express

You can create Reels, flyers, TikTok videos, resumes, logos, banners, and even more with the recent all-one Adobe's Express application for a quicker and faster way for creating contents.

Explore the limitless possibilities using Adobe Express.

- Mix video clips, works of art, music and animations, to create videos using the drag & drop ease.
- Finish one-click projects with Adobe Photo, Adobe's video, design, & PDF tools at your disposal.
- Using Adobe's Firefly generative AI, you can create amazing text effects and pictures quickly from a brief description.
- With thousands of expertly created templates, Adobe videos, music, Adobe Stock photos, and even more, finish designs more quickly.
- Work together as a team and provide real-time feedback on files.
- Access & insert linked Adobe Illustrator and Photoshop assets with ease, ensuring they are constantly in sync.

Combine video clips, artwork, animations, and music to make videos with drag-and-drop ease.

Get to know about our community

Get the most recent feature announcements, creative advice, tutorials, and unique information. Interact with other users. Share your thoughts. Seek guidance. Stay in touch with the Adobe Express customer service team.

Uncover all of Adobe Express incredible features.

Here's a sneak peek at some of the amazing features of Adobe Express that can help you create content that stands out.

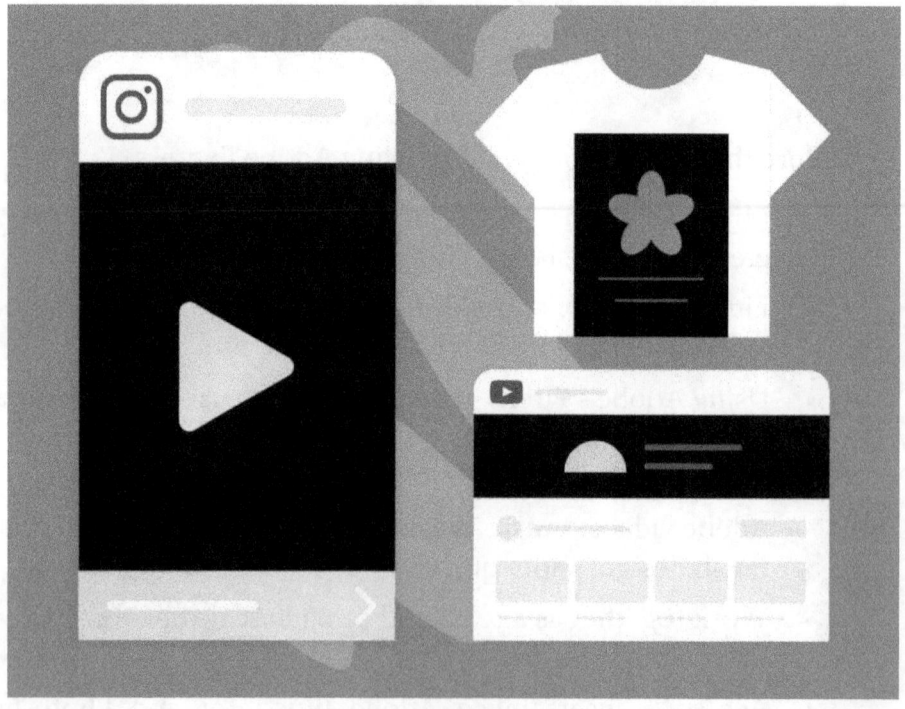

Video creation

You can create Reels & TikToks swiftly and effortlessly using your drag-&-drop videos creation. Using templates or your personalized static designs as a startin g point, add your logo, creative assets, music and videos from Adobe Stock, and more.

Generative AI tools

With generative AI tools, you can create designs more quickly and efficiently by eliminating the need for guesswork. Adobe's Firefly generative AI allows you to generate amazing text effects & images instantaneously from a brief description.

Expertly designed templates

Instantly begin working with the free, expertly designed video as well as several-pages templates, along with all-new Stock videos of Adobe and music. With just a couple of clicks, you can add content to any template to make it uniquely yours.

Single-click tasks

You can use the Quick Actions for speeding up your workflow. Professional Adobe features available in Adobe's Express can be used with just one click: editing PDFs, resizing photos and videos, removing backgrounds, and trimming video clips.

Cost of an Adobe Express membership

For mobile and web applications, Adobe's Express Free is free.

The Adobe Express Premier plan provides the complete version the Adobe Express application, containing all the premium features as well as allows you construct branded stories using your logo, fonts and colours. The vast majority of the Adobe Creative Cloud's plans come with it, or you can purchase it separately via the Adobe websites through in-apps purchases on mobile apps, or as part of a stand-alone subscription.

Adobe Express for Teams, Enterprise, and Education

For Education

With features created specifically for the educational setting, Adobe Express for Education—which includes Photoshop Express and Adobe Express which is free for educators and students to use while adhering to Adobe's usual data privacy standards.

Express for Education is available to universities and colleges that have Adobe Creative Cloud's Apps for Higher Education installed.

It's easier to foster effective creative experiences for learning with Adobe Express. Adobe Express can be used by educators and students for creating picture essays, student portfolios, trip reports, school newsletters, sports announcements, and other content.

For teams & enterprises

Purchases of Adobe Express product can now be made independently. Purchase Express by Adobe for Teams to get started right away for small and medium-sized enterprises.

For bigger enterprise enterprises requiring enterprise-level safety and integrations, discover more and reach out to sales.

Getting the Adobe Express

You may employ Adobe Express in your mobile devices and on the internet.

1. Go to the Adobe Express website.
2. Install Adobe Express in the devices you own: Android | iOS

You can check out system's requirements to determine the bare minimum of technical specifications needed for creating graphics and content on your devices.

Important:

Use your Creative Cloud login information to log in if you are a subscriber to Adobe's Creative Cloud. In this manner, the applications will be available to you in their entirety.

Adobe Express System Requirements

- Adobe Express on web
- Adobe Express on mobile
- Adobe Express on mobile (beta)

Adobe Express on the web

Find out the bare minimum system & technical specifications for generating content with Adobe Express in your desktop internet and in supported languages.

Hint:

Make sure your gadgets are connected to internet, to make use of your Adobe Express

Operating Systems	**Windows:** Version 10 or later **macOS:** Version 11 or later **ChromeOS**
Web browsers	**Google Chrome:** Version 100 and onwards **Microsoft Edge:** Version 107 and onwards **Safari:** Version 16 and onwards **Firefox:** Version 117 and onwards **Note:** JavaScript must be enabled
Memory requirements	Minimum 4GB memory
Hardware acceleration	Check if hardware acceleration is enabled in your browser. Read more about **enabling hardware acceleration**.
WebGL2	Navigate to the **WebGL Report** and ensure you get a green check mark, saying your browser supports WebGL2.
WebAssembly	Navigate to the **WebAssembly page** and check if you get a purple screen saying your browser supports WebAssembly.

Important:

Your browser does not fulfil our minimum requirements if it is unable to pass the Web Assembly and WebGL2 requirements.

Technical requirements

This is applicable for the Adobe Express in iOS, Android and web.

When uploading images into the Adobe Express editor, the following specifications are met.

Formats accepted	JPG, PNG
Maximum resolution at import	8k x 8k
Maximum size at import	40MB
Maximum number of images that can be uploaded to a single page of a file	100

Quick action image requirements

When using Adobe Express in the web & Adobe Express for Android and iOS devices to edit images (for instance, Removing Background, Resizing Image), the requirements that follow must be met.

Formats accepted	JPG, PNG
Maximum resolution at import	4k x 4k
Maximum size at import	17MB

Language versions available

The following languages are supported by Adobe Express:

- English
- Chinese - simplified
- Chinese - traditional
- Danish
- Dutch
- Finnish
- French
- Italian
- Japanese
- Korean
- Norwegian
- Spanish
- Swedish
- German
- Brazilian Portuguese
- Welsh

Keyboard Shortcuts

Learn all of the built-in keyboard shortcuts, tricks, and tips to expedite basic app workflow as well as tasks involving the editing of images and videos.

Hint:

These keyboard shortcuts are exclusive to the graphic creation. These might not be relevant if you're creating a webpage or videos.

Common Actions

Result	macOS	Windows
Confirm text entry	Shift + Return	Shift + Enter
Duplicate & place	Option + drag	Alt + drag
Undo	Cmd + Z	Ctrl + Z
Redo	Cmd + Shift + Z Cmd + Y	Ctrl + Shift + Z Ctrl + Y

Move, Rotate & Arrange

Result	macOS	Windows
Nudge 1px. up, down, left, or right	Arrow keys	Arrow keys
Nudge 10px up, down, left, or right	Shift + Arrow keys	Shift + Arrow keys
Rotate 1° clockwise	Option + Right arrow	Alt + Right arrow
Rotate 1° counterclockwise	Option + Left arrow	Alt + Left arrow
Rotate 15° clockwise	Option + Shift + Right arrow	Alt + Shift + Right arrow
Rotate 15° counterclockwise	Option + Shift + Left arrow	Alt + Shift + Left arrow
Bring forward	Cmd +]	Ctrl +]
Bring to front	Cmd + Option +]	Ctrl + Alt +]
Send backward	Cmd + [	Ctrl + [
Send to back	Cmd + Option + [	Ctrl + Alt + [
Distribute Horizontal	Command + Ctrl + H	Ctrl + Alt + H
Distribute Vertical	Command + Ctrl + V	Ctrl + Alt + V

Selection

Result	macOS	Windows
Select multiple	Shift + Click	Shift + Click
Marquee select	Cmd + drag	Ctrl + drag
Select all	Cmd + A	Ctrl + A
Deselect all	Cmd + Shift + A	Ctrl + Shift + A

Select none	Esc	Esc
Add / Remove from existing selection	Shift + Click	Shift + Click

Grouping

Result	macOS	Windows
Group	Cmd + G	Ctrl + G
Ungroup	Cmd + Shift + G	Ctrl + Shift + G
Select a level up in a group	Esc	Esc
Select a level down in a group	Shift + Esc	Shift + Esc
Select the next item in a group	Tab	Tab
Select the previous item in a group	Shift + Tab	Shift + Tab

Zoom

Result	macOS	Windows
Zoom in	Cmd + + Cmd + mousewheel* Pinch out on trackpad**	Ctrl + + Ctrl + mousewheel* Pinch out on trackpad**
Zoom out	Cmd + - Cmd + mousewheel* Pinch in on trackpad**	Ctrl + - Ctrl + mousewheel* Pinch out on trackpad**
Fit in window	Cmd + 0	Ctrl + 0
Fill in window	Cmd + Shift + 0	n/a
View in actual size / 100%	Cmd + Option + 0	Ctrl + Alt + 0

Zoom in to cursor position	Spacebar + Cmd + click	Spacebar + Ctrl + click
Zoom out from cursor position	Spacebar + Option + click	Spacebar + Alt + click
Pan / Move canvas	Spacebar + drag Arrow key while zoomed in with nothing is selected (hold arrow key to speed up) Page up/down Slide with 2 fingers on trackpad	Spacebar + drag Arrow key while zoomed in with nothing is selected (hold arrow key to speed up) Page up/down Slide with 2 fingers on trackpad

Edit video

Result	macOS	Windows
Play / Pause Timeline	Space	Space
Copy videos	Cmd + C	Ctrl + C
Paste videos	Cmd + V	Ctrl + V
Duplicate videos	Cmd + D	Ctrl + D
Delete videos	Delete	Delete
Split scene (Scene to be selected)	S	S
Delete scene (Scene to be selected)	Delete	Delete
Duplicate scene (Scene to be selected)	Cmd + D	Ctrl + D
Split audio (Audio to be selected)	S	S
Mute audio (Audio to be selected)	M	M
Deleted audio (Audio to be selected)	Delete	Delete
Duplicate Audio (Audio to be selected)	Cmd + D	Ctrl + D

Edit text

Action description	macOS	Windows
Bold Text	Command + B	Ctrl + B
Italicize Text	Command + I	Ctrl + I
Underline Text	Command + U	Ctrl + U
Increase Font Size	Command + shift + .	Ctrl + shift + .
Decrease Font Size	Command + shift + ,	Ctrl + shift + ,
Text Align Left	Option + shift + L	Alt + shift + L
Text Align Right	Option + shift + R	Alt + shift + R
Text Align Center	Option + shift + C	Alt + shift + C
Edit selected text object	Press Enter while text object is selected to activate cursor	Press Enter while text object is selected to activate cursor

Using the Command/Control + mousewheel gesture is going to zoom your entire browser when your pointer is positioned outside of canvas in some browsers.

The Pinch for zooming gesture with the use of trackpad currently is not supported in Safari.

Some shortcuts aren't supported on the Microsoft Edge. We suggest switching into Firefox or Chrome to fully use these shortcuts.

Progressive Web Application

Installing the Progressive Web Application

You should install Adobe Express desktops application as your Progressive Web Application (PWA).

In order to simulate the experience of a natively application, Progressive Web Apps (PWAs) are browser-based applications that are developed and delivered through the internet with app-like interfaces. Adobe Express serves as a web-enabled application that lacks any companion desktop app; however, you may install your Adobe Express desktop app as your native application on your computer, such as Chromebooks.

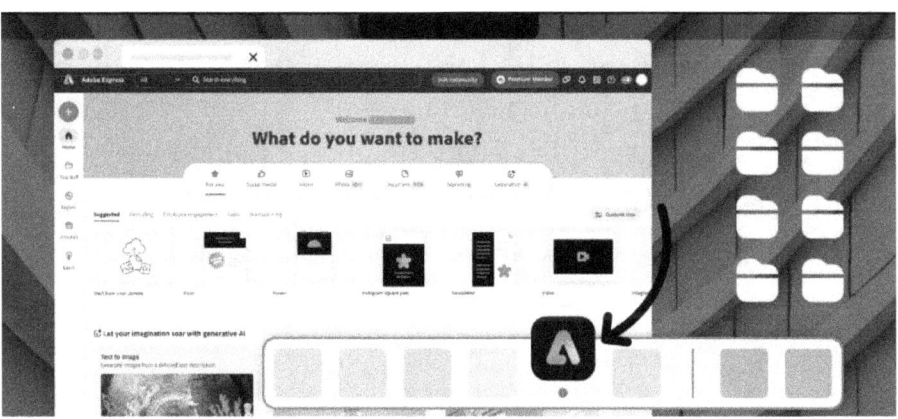

Benefits of the Progressive Web Apps (PWA)

- It is easy to install.
- It response excellently well and loads really fast.
- It can easily be accessible from your taskbar in any Windows device or your Dock in the Mac device.

Installing your Adobe Express PWAs

- Microsoft application store for any Windows device
- Chrome browsers
- Edge browsers

Hint:

As at present, Firefox and Safari browsers doesn't support the installation of PWAs.

Effortlessly accessing your Adobe Express Progressive Web App

- **In your Windows device**: You should right-click on your Adobe Express ⬛ icon then choose **the Shows more options** > then tap Pin to taskbar.
- **In your Mac device**: You should right-click on your Adobe's Express ⬛ icon then you tap on **Options** > then select **Keep in dock**.

ADDING THE ADOBE EXPRESS BROWSER EXTENSION

Install your Adobe Express extension on your Google Chrome browsers to easily edit photos to your ideal specifications.

Installing your Adobe Express Chrome extension

1. Access your chrome's web store.
2. From your Search section, you should enter in Adobe Express then choose your extension.
3. Choose the **Adds to Chrome** > then tap **Add extension**.

Pining your extension on your browser toolbar

The extension can be quickly accessed by pinning it onto your browser toolbar after installation.

1. You should select your **Extensions** 🧩 icon which is toward your right of your address bar in order to open your extensions dropdown.
2. You should select your **Pin** icon which is next to the Adobe Express.

After it's pinned on your browser, use your Adobe's Express ▲ extension for designing creations and do quick operations by navigating to the right-side of your address bar.

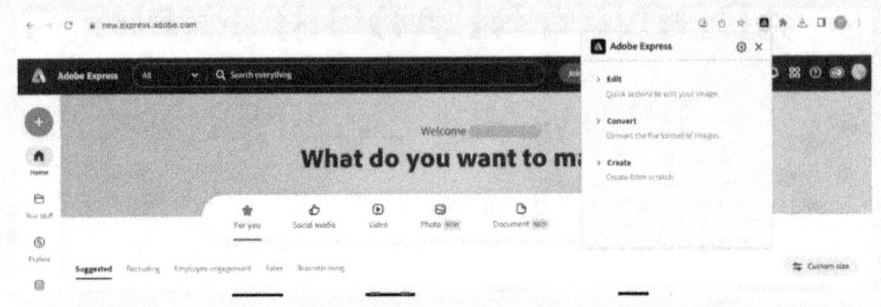

You should select Adobe's Express extension on the right side of your address bar then choose a task

Launching your Adobe Express extension

After your Adobe Express web browser extension is installed, you can quickly perform quick actions or make creative modifications by just right-clicking on an image from the internet to open your Adobe's Express editor. To make use of the extension, make sure you're logged in with a legitimate Adobe ID.

Editing your image

1. You should select your image from the web then you right-click upon it.

2. You should select your **Edit with Adobe Express** > then tap on **Create a New project to launch** your Express editor on that same window.

3. Then edit your image then tap on **Download**.

Using your images quick actions

1. You should select your image from the web then you right-click it.

2. You should select your **Edits with Adobe Express** and then choose any of the below quick actions:

- Crop image
- Remove background
- Resize image
- Convert to JPG
- Convert to PNG

3. Choose **Download / Continue in Adobe Express.**

Most commonly asked questions
When I attempt to open the extension, I receive an error message. What should I do after that?

To troubleshoot your error message below adhere to these steps below:

- Navigate to your browser Settings > then select Privacy & security > then tap on Third party cookies > then select Allow third party cookies

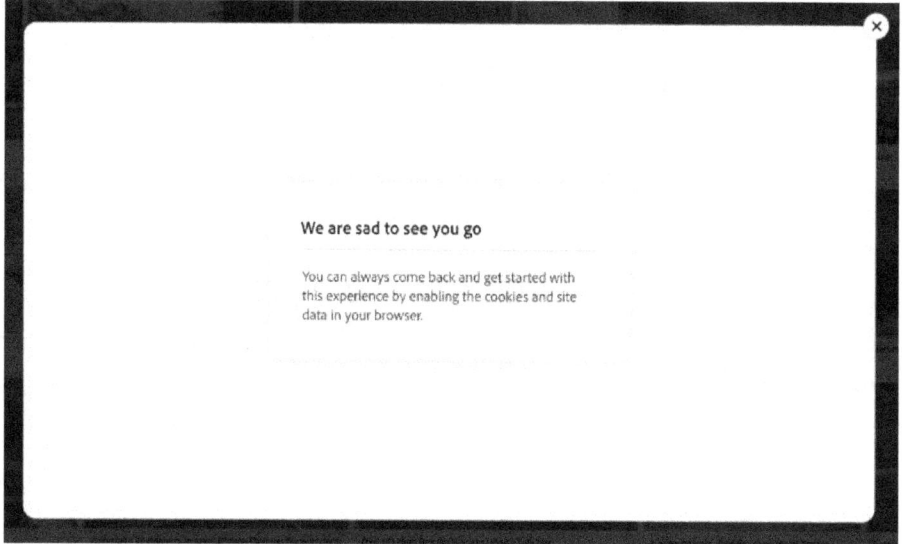

Error notification

How will I save image that is edited on Adobe's Express web files?

The modifications to images with Quick actions / Create from scratch automatically are saved in the Express web files. These can be found in your Adobe's Express Google Chrome Extension folder.

If I don't type a URL into my address bar, will my pinned view still work?

No, your pinned view will not work when you do not have any URL type in on your address bar. Enter in your URL of your choice then try out your pinned view.

When I try to modify an image or do a quick action, why am I receiving an error warning (Unknown error)?

On these two scenarios, you are going to receive an **Unknown error**:

- Whenever you are making use of unsupported versions of browsers, these are versions of Chrome below 100.
- Whenever you don't have a network connectivity.

When I attempt to use my Adobe Express's extension with my Enterprise account, a blocked screen appears. How do I open the extension on my end?

When you've got any Enterprise account, you are going to see a blocked screen when you do not possess Adobe's Express entitlement on the Enterprise account you own. You can reach out to (contact) the admin of your Enterprise for access.

MOBILE APP

Adobe Express mobile beta overview

The Adobe Express serves as an all-in-one AI contents creation application for creating videos, social posts, flyers, and many more. The latest mobile application is available now in beta. You should share your views to make this application better. We appreciate you for helping us mould the future of the Adobe Express. Thank you for shaping the future of Adobe Express.

Scaning the QR code to get started on mobile

- Use your to scan QR code to view your eligibility.
- Check out the list for eligible devices.

Verify your eligibility & get started

Android users

- Download your Adobe Express mobile application (beta) for your Android.
- Beta is accessible in eligible devices, going out to more devices, which includes tablets, over time.

iOS users

- Join the waitlist for the iOS beta application. We've put you on a waitlist since Apple has established a 10,000 user restriction for Testflight.
- The beta is accessible on compatible smartphones and will gradually roll out to other devices—including tablets.

GENERATE AND EDIT GRAPHICS, VIDEOS AND PHOTOS

Working with Adobe Illustrator and Photoshop creative assets

Effortlessly work with your linked Adobe's Illustrator and Photoshop creative assets within Adobe Express.

Add assets from your Adobe Photoshop & Adobe Illustrator to your Express designs. With a Linked Asset, all edits performed in your Illustrator or Photoshop will be updated on your Adobe Express designs, this there means you are always in sync.

Adding Linked Asset

1. On your editor, go to your **Media** pane then choose **Upload from device**.
2. In your device, look for any Photoshop / Illustrator file.
3. Then move & resize your **Linked Asset** inside your editor then you can add text, photo, filters, and even more.

Editing Linked Asset

1. From your editor, choose your linked file which you would like to edit.
2. Then choose **Open in Illustrator / Open in Photoshop** from your **Linked Asset** for opening your appropriate program, based on the type of file.

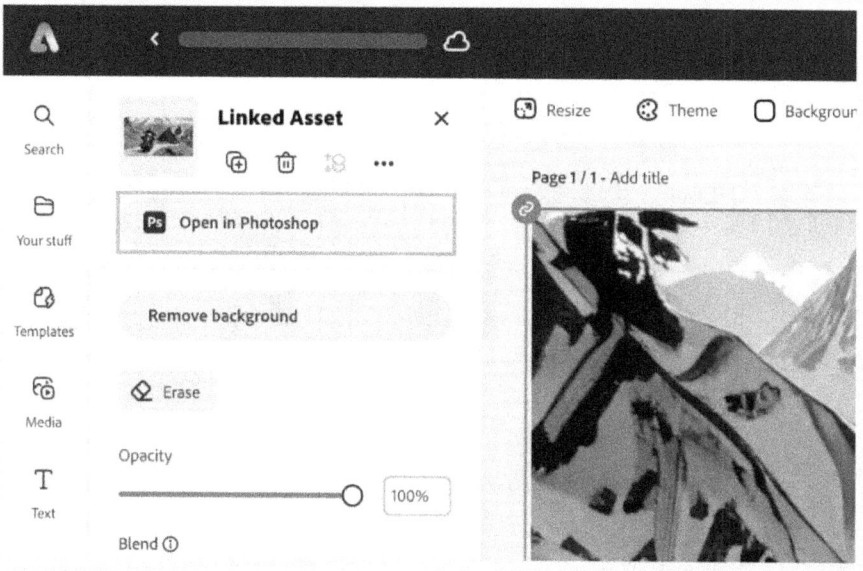

You should choose Open in Illustrator / Open in Photoshop underneath Linked Asset to open your appropriate program.

3. Edit and save your changes within Illustration or Photoshop, then go to your Adobe Express. You are going to see this message, "Your linked assets have changed" on your monitor. Choose **Update** to see your changes & then resync your file.

Importing your file

1. From your homepage, from the Get started, you should choose Start from your content.

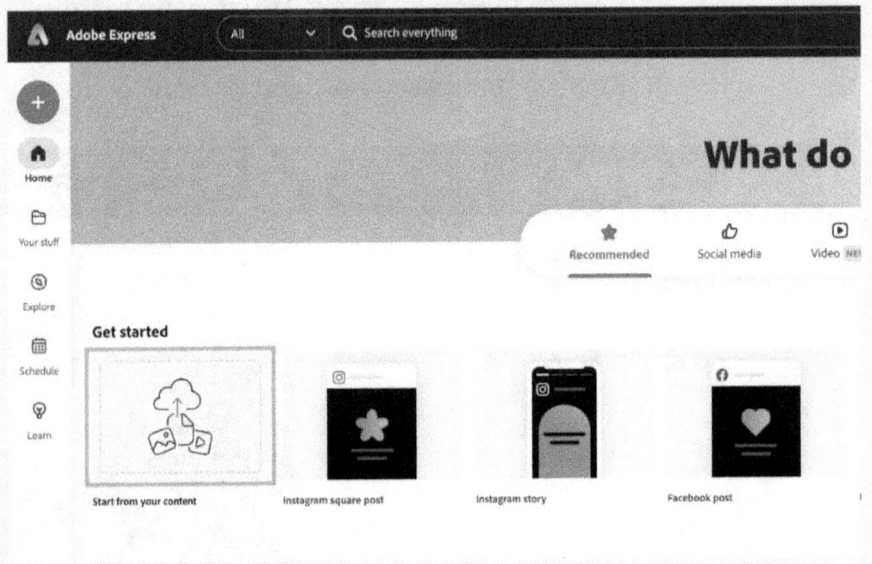

Choose Start from your content from your homepage of Express for importing your Illustrator / Photoshop files.

2. Look for any Illustrator or Photoshop file in your device. After uploaded, you should choose **Open in editor**.

3. Then makes your edits in your editor. Then **Download / Share** after edited.

IMPORTING AND ENHANCING PDFS WITHIN ADOBE EXPRESS

Discover how to add captivating text, graphics, branding, colours, animations, & more to PDFs to improve them.

You can import your PDF files, like flyers, brochures and even more, as your editable Express files and then enhance it via inserting design assets. Check out this example of how to reuse a marketing PDF brochure by importing it into Adobe Express.

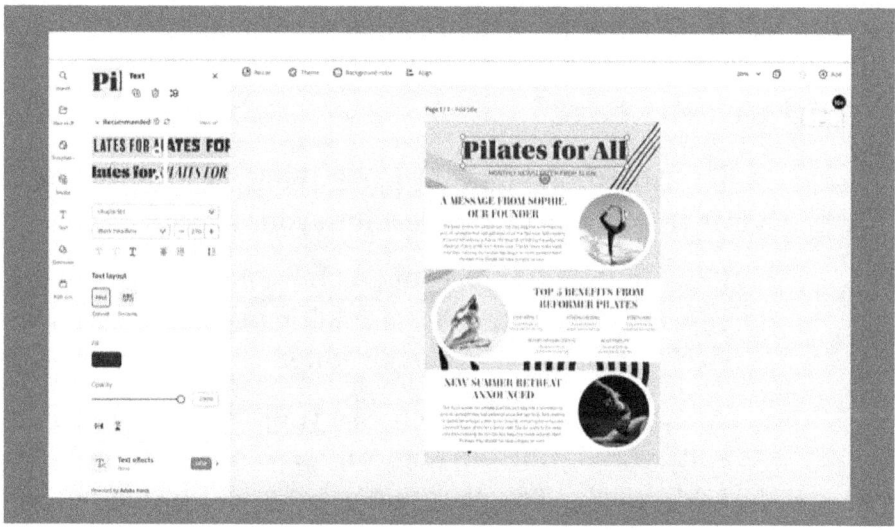

Importing PDF file to your Adobe Express

1. From your homepage of your Adobe Express, underneath **Get started**, choose the **Start from your content**.
2. Look for any PDF within your device then choose the **Open in editor**.

Enhance PDF files

Adding or replacing images

1. Select Media from your left pane to add a picture into your PDF file.
2. Choose **Upload from device** to use Text to picture generative AI to create an image, search through your Adobe Stock images, or upload file in your device.
3. Choose the image in your PDF file to be replaced, then click your **Replace** ⇋ icon to replace any image.

Add or edit text

1. Select **Text** from your left pane, then you choose **the Add your text,** to insert new text into your PDF.

    2. Enter in your text on your text box and then format it with your styling options on your left pane, your fonts, colour, size and many more can be edited.

    3. For your text edition, choose your from your PDF, then edit with your styling options on your left pane. Additionally, you can animate your text by making use of the **Animation** in your left pane.

Adding assets, logos, & more

1. You should choose **Elements** ◈ on your left pane to inserts Design assets, **Shapes**, **Backgrounds**, or **Icons** into the PDF file.
2. Choose the **Your stuff** > then select **Brands and Libraries** to include your **Logos**, **Fonts**, **brand Colours**, and **Graphics**.

Adding pages

You can easily add a new page to create a cover page or table of contents for your brochure.

1. Choose the **Templates** on your left pane.
2. Look through your templates or you use ▽ it to streamline your results.
3. Choose a template then you select **Add as pages** from your pop-up.

Hint:

Add text effects to elevate your design on an entirely new level. Give your clients access to your magnificent new PDF.

GETTING STARTED WITH THE ADOBE EXPRESS TEMPLATES

Thousands of expertly designed and customized templates are accessible from Adobe Express for all of your marketing and social media requirements. Create and customize stunning flyers, presentations, videos, carousels, social media posts, and more by exploring with templates.

Getting started with template

1. From your Adobe Express homepage, hover over any task in your top row, then choose the **Browse templates** to launch your editor & view templates.

2. Then scroll through your templates or choose ▽ to narrow down your results on Videos, Animated templates, or Multiple page.

3. In your left pane, choose the **Text** > then tap **Add your text** to insert new text into your template. Enter your text on your text box then format it with your styli ng options available in your left pane. Additionally, you can edit & style your already existing text in your template.

4. In your left pane, choose the **Media** to insert **Photos / Videos**, all dependent on what you'd like to create. Select the **Upload from device** / you look through your library to include a video or photo to the template.

5. Make use of your layers pane to choose your photo or video which you would like to replace on your template, then tap on **Replace** ⇄.

6. You should add animation on your text & images to make it look nicer.

7. Choose the **Elements** ◊ within your left pane to insert **Design Assets, Shapes, Backgrounds** and **Icons**.

8. Choose **Theme** for editing your colours then choose the Background colour to put **background colour** on your template.

9. Then **Download** the template to your device or choose **Share** to display your product to the public.

What comes next?

You may quickly and easily construct a template for social media graphics, logos, flyers and many more using Adobe Express.

CREATING NEW TEMPLATE FROM SCRATCH

You can use Adobe Express for creating unique templates of social graphics, logos, flyers, and many other from scratch.

Create a fresh template from starting.

1. On your Adobe Express homepage, hover over your task on your top row, then choose **Create from scratch**.
2. You can create your own unique designs with these following options on your left pane.

Design	Description
Search	Select **Search** to search for the design assets you want to insert in your template. Once you select the photos or videos, you can select it and it'll be on the blank canvas.
Your Stuff	Select **Your stuff** to easily apply fonts, colours, and logos to any file from a brand you've created or shared.
Templates	Select **Templates** to create and personalize beautiful social posts, videos, carousels, flyers, and presentations that can be added to your blank canvas.
Media	Select **Media** to add new photos, videos, or audio to the template. Choose from the photo library or select Upload from the device to add.
Text	Select **Text** to add text to the template. Type your text in the text box and format it using the available styling options from the left panel. You can also edit and style the existing text on the template.
Elements	Select **Elements** to add **Design Assets**, **Backgrounds**, **Shapes**, and **Icons**.
Add-ons	Select **Add-ons** to bring the third-party app designs into the template.

3. After finishing, you may **Share** or **Download** your design on various social media channels.

What comes next?

By adding many pages, you may utilize Adobe Express to create visually appealing and captivating social graphics and Instagram carousels. It will support your business growth and audience connection.

CREATING WEBPAGE WITH ADOBE EXPRESS

Create, share, and host, a single-paged webpage with Adobe Express.

You can create single-paged website pages for your portfolios, presentations, resumes, photo galleries, blog posts, and even more. These web pages can also serve as a business's monthly or weekly newsletter, a display for your product catalog, or an advertisement for an exclusive offer.

Creating your webpage

1. In your Adobe Express homepage, choose ⊕.
2. In **Create**, choose the **Webpage**.
3. Add your title & subtitle to your webpage. Add your **Photo** 🖼, your **Short Cover** 📇, & **Split Layout** 🗔.
4. Then tap on **Themes** ✨ in order to apply the theme of your choice and then specify the **Fonts & Styles** of your webpage.

5. Then insert Photos, Text, Videos, Buttons, Photo Grid, Glideshow, and Split layout on your webpage so that your brand will look spectacular.

Insert design assets into your webpage

6. In your header, tap text box for rename your webpage.

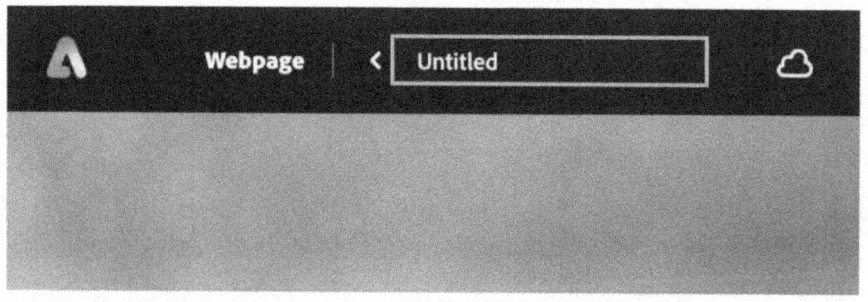

Tap Text box for renaming wepage.

7. Swiftly carry out these actions while you are making edit on your webpage.

↶: Undo your action.

↷: Redo your action.

✨ : Change the theme.

◉ : Check the preview.

▷: Present your webpage.

8. After you finish your webpage, tap on **Share** > then select **Publish to web** > then select **Create link** to acquire your new, exclusive URL.

Important:

When you make edit on your webpage, you should republish it to allow your updates go live & your URL doesn't change.

Hint:

The **Share** tool can also generate a snippet of code that allows you to embed your new page into an existing website by pasting the code into your site files.

Adding various visual assets on your webpage

Set up design theme for your web page by using your photos, logos, icons, customized fonts, and additional customizable elements in order to make them appear entirely authentic.

Assets	Description
Photos	You can search for free photos from Adobe Stock or bring them in from your Libraries, Lightroom, Dropbox, Google Photos, and Google Drive. You can also add GIFs from Giphy or Tenor.
Text	Add your text and adjust the format and alignment. Assign H1 or H2 components to make a heading. You can also add hyperlinks to your text.
Button	Add button text and assign a URL.
Videos	Add a YouTube video or Vimeo.
Photo grid	Add multiple photos to build your grid. You can move around the photos and adjust their size.
Glideshow	Upload photos, add text, block quotes, images, and more in a block component to give you a new way to tell your story.
Split layout	You can split your webpage into two halves by selecting **Split layout**. Once done, add photos, text, buttons, and videos.

Adding custom themes to a webpage

Tap on your **Themes** icon, then choose **Create a theme**. Adjust your background colour, font, and more on the **Edit theme** pane in order to add custom theme on your webpage.

ADDING MULTIPLE PAGES TO ADOBE EXPRESS FILES

Add several pages of whatever size in one file with Adobe Express. Quickly & effortlessly develop campaigns having a consistent appearance and feel throughout your TikTok, Instagram, digital advertisements, and more simply via working on the pages of all size, all inside your same file.

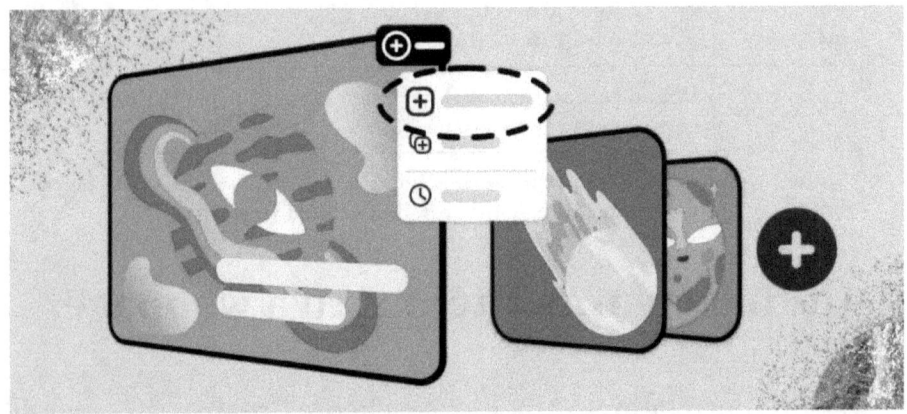

Getting started with the multiple pages

1. In your Adobe Express homepage, choose a template or start from scratch.

2. Choose **Add** ⊕ to select and **Add new page** option on your editor. Otherwise, choose **Resize** on your header, then you **Duplicate & resize** a design to make fresh assets for marketing campaign, all inside a single file.

   Important: You may include up to 99 pages in just one file.

3. Tap **Share** for inviting collaborators / schedule your post.

Hint:

- View every of your pages at a glance. Use your **View all pages** key for reviewing your designs, then you double-click any page to keep on editing.

- Use your **Delete page** 🗑 icon in the top right of the toolbar to delete a page from the project.

What comes next?

Invite your team to collaborate on your designs in real time. Post comments, tag team members, and resolve comments all-in-one place to help you stay organized and work together efficiently.

CREATE VIDEO WITH ADOBE EXPRESS

You can craft fascinating videos with Adobe Express.

With the drag-&-drop video creation, you can currently easily and quickly generate unique videos using templates as well as custom static designs, & you can effortlessly modify the timing for individual objects so that your content come to life. You may add your design assets, brand, music, & videos from Adobe Stock, among other things.

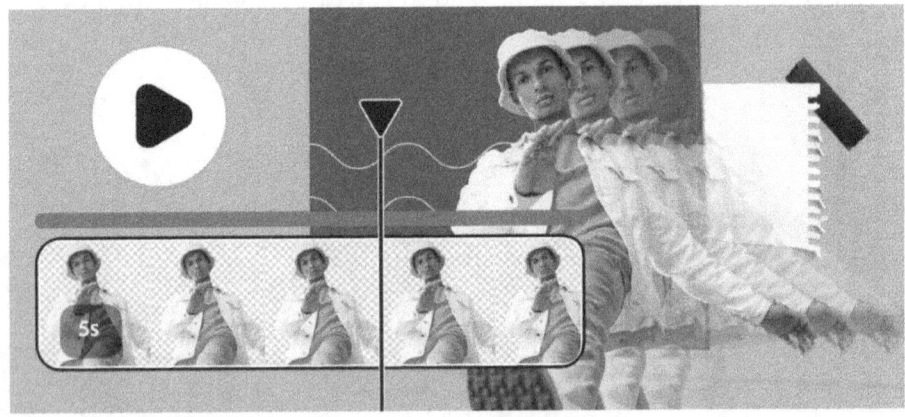

Getting started with video

1. On your homepage, tap **Video** from your **What do you want to make**. Hover over a video task that you like and then tap on **Create from scratch**.

2. Choose **Upload from device** or search your Adobe Stock photos / videos.

3. Choose a video from your page to launch your left pane with the options for crop, adjust your volume & speed, or you add animations, filters, and more.

4. Select **Text** if you would like to add text into your video or **Elements** to add, backgrounds, shapes, and more.

5. Tap **Media** > then select **Audio** to add music, or select **Record voiceover** to make your own recording.

Adding scenes into your timeline

Video scenes serve as containers for your contents, and they can hold text, graphics, videos, and images.

1. Choose **Add scene** from right of your timeline to insert a new scene, or you simply drag & drop video, images, and more into your timeline.

2. Hover on your scene to expose your trim handles & drag on them to lengthen or shorten the time for your videos scenes.

Adjust timing of any layer in your video

Any object in your page can have its time adjusted in a video by selecting it.

1. To view your chosen layer, tap **Show layer timing** within your timeline.
2. To show the trim handles, hover over your layer track's starting or ending. Drag them to change the object's duration from short to long.

Locate your timed objects in any scene

Objects in your video, including text, graphics, and design components, are easy to identify. These objects can be placed more strategically by making use of the timing indication dots.

Select your timing indicator dot for adjusting the timing of your object

1. After you've timed your layer, you are going to see dots, each one of it represents the starting time of the object on your video.
2. Hover above any dot to see the thumbnail for that object.
3. Choose the thumbnail to pull up your layer timeline.
4. Drag your trim handles in order to increase or decrease the duration for your object within your video.

Hint:

You may drag your trim handle in your track then alter it to be the exact starting point or ending point as that of a different layer on your video.

Adjusting timing of your audio track

1. Once you have added your audio, choose your purple track underneath your timeline pane to edit your audio track.
2. Then drag your purple track along your timeline to specify when your audio track will start.
3. Then hover over your purple timeline to disclose your trim handles then drag them for increasing or decreasing the duration for your audio track.

Important:

You should Submit your content ID code when you get copyright claim while uploading your video into YouTube which employs Adobe's Stock music track.

FINDING AND SUBMITING ADOBE STOCK CONTENT ID

Find your Content ID code for your Adobe's Stock music tracks made in the Adobe Express & use it for responding to copyright demands on YouTube.

Using Adobe Express, hundreds of Adobe's stock soundtracks can be accessed and then added to your videos. A Content ID and license code may be required whenever uploading any video on YouTube. To assist copyright holders in protecting their music, YouTube employs Contents ID technology. YouTube automatically looks for music that matches videos you submit to your channel within its Content Identification (ID) database. You might receive copyright claim if it discovers a match.

You must send your **Content ID** code for every Adobe's Stock music track used in your video if you get any copyright claim on YouTube for any of your video that features music from your Adobe stock.

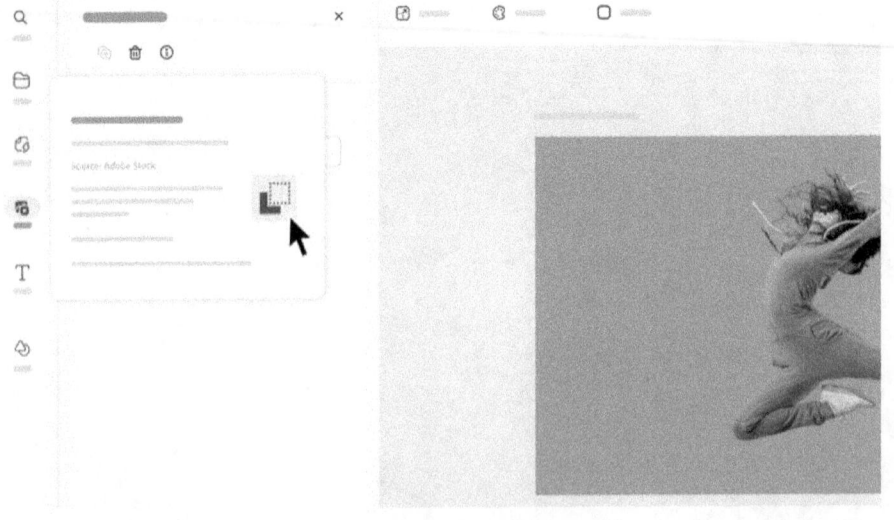

1. After you have created your videos on Adobe Express, you should choose **Download** for exporting.

2. Once it downloaded, choose your Adobe Stock sound track layer employ for your video.

3. Choose your **Source** ⓘ**Info** symbol to see your exclusive **Content ID code**.

4. Then copy your **Content ID** code into your clipboard via selecting your **Copy** icon beside it.

5. Then you submit your Content ID code to YouTube to erase your copyright claim.

Attention:

Type in code only used for your music track on your video. Do not input another codes / text to prevent delays in freeing your video.

ANIMATE PHOTOS, TEXT, AND VIDEOS ON ADOBE EXPRESS

Use Adobe Express to animate text, images, and videos to give your projects more energy.

Adding animation on any element of your design—text, images, and even videos—will help your content come to life. Three primary types of animation are available: **In**, **Looping**, & **Out**. Easily adjust the time of the animation's appearance in your design by customizing its direction, speed, & other options.

Animate text, photos and videos

1. In your editor, choose text, an image or a video for your design.
2. Choose **Animation** by swiping down in your left pane.
3. Choose one or several creative animation options from **In**, **Out**, & **Looping**, then adjust it's speed, timing, personality, & even more

In

This causes text to appear on your design a letter per a time, make your photo zoom in from the outside, & do much 111 more, with **In** animation.

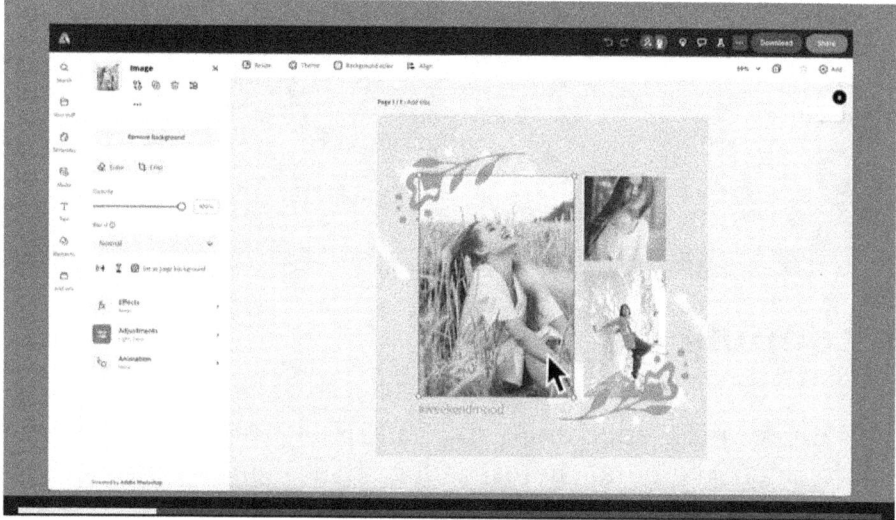

Out

With **Out** animation, you can use it for making text disappear a single letter per a time, zoom out a photo to expose new image, & much more.

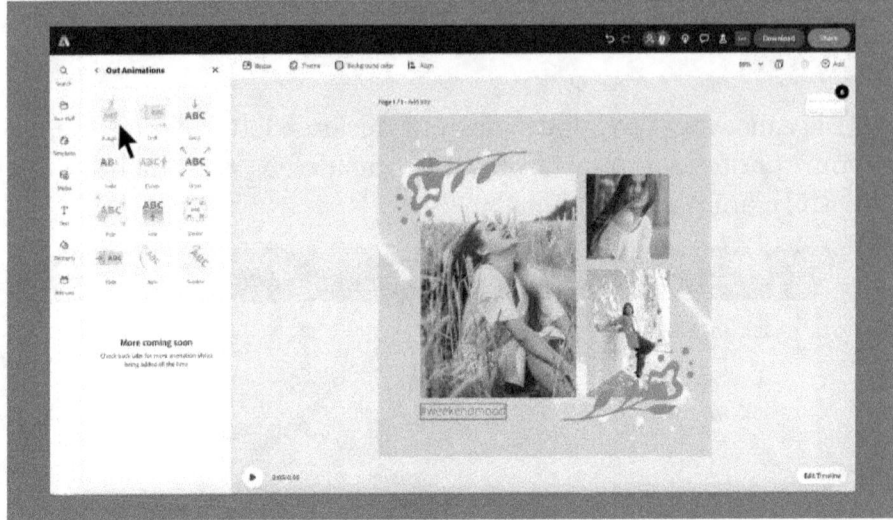

Looping

With **looping** animation, you can use it to create a constantly moving background, animate a logo that bounces up & down, and a lot more.

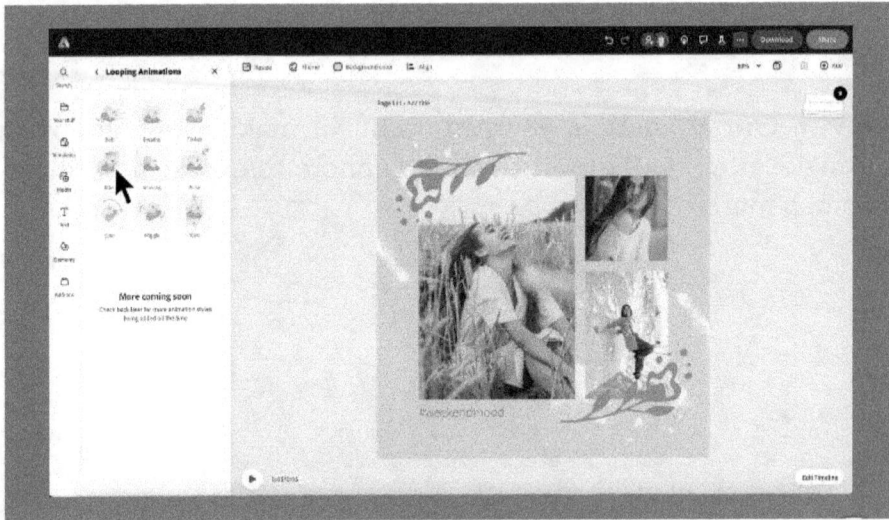

What comes next?

You can employ Adobe Express's app to make animated social media postings that will amaze your audience if you put a bit of creativity into it. Therefore, why do you delay? Begin to utilize animated images and text on your network's posts!

IMPORTING COLOUR THEMES INTO ADOBE EXPRESS

Import colour themes from your Adobe Colour into Adobe's Express for all of your content.

Open your Adobe Colour app and adhere to these steps:

1. You should tap on **Trends**, **Explore**, or **Libraries** at the header for opening theme view of any other theme.

2. Choose any of your colour swatch for automatically copy your hex colour code.

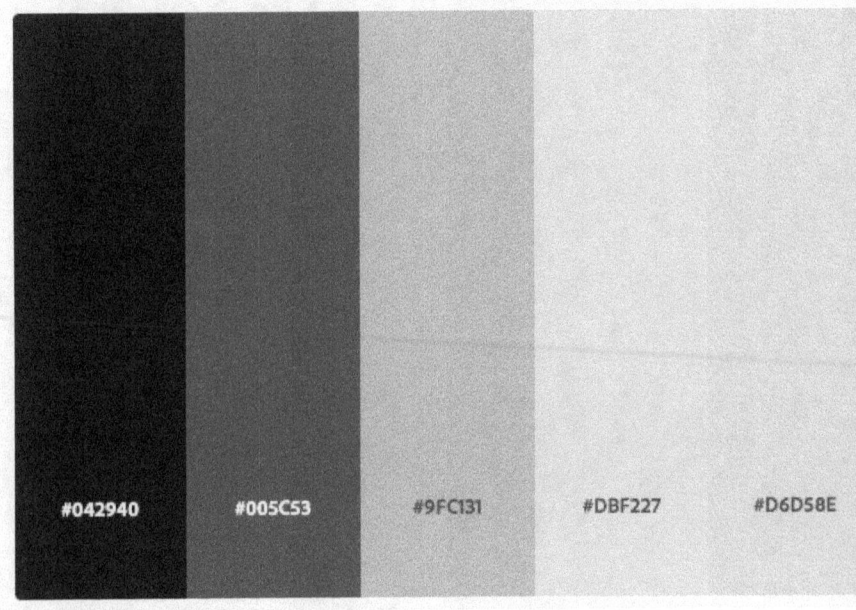

Copy hex colour code from swatch

3. Launch any file on Adobe Express then choose **Your stuff** from your left pane.

4. Tap on **Brands & Libraries** then go to your library to which you would like to add colours.

5. From your **Colours** dropdown, tap **Colours** > then select **Add your colours** to launch your colour editing tools then tap on **Custom**.

6. choose and highlight your existing hex value, comprising the #, paste your new hex code, & tap **Save**.

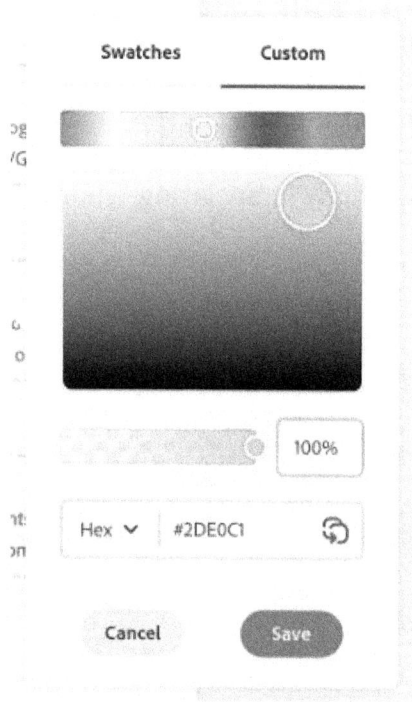

To import more colours, repeat steps 2-6.

TRANSLATE YOUR FILES AND YOUR TEMPLATES

You can translate files on the Adobe Express with just few clicks.

By effectively translating your text on single & multi-page files into your selection of 46 languages, you can do away with the necessity for manually translating and the headaches associated with using third-party translation tools. In addition, you may utilize the large library of English templates via translating your text into the languages of your choice.

Important:

Translate is a premium feature and is available for free only for a limited period of time.

Translate content

1. Open Adobe Express and select a file / template which needs to be translated into another language. Choose Translate from the menu at top of your editor page.

2. Your **Translate** page pane's **From** dropdown detects your source language automatically. To select one or more target languages, open your To dropdown menu.
3. Choose **Duplicate and translate**

Commonly asked questions

How is the Translate feature implemented?

Translate feature offers a translation automatically based on the language you wrote in. A third-party engine called Google Translate powers this service.

The language in my file differs from the detected source language. How should I proceed?

You can manually choose the source language from the From dropdown when your auto-detected languages fails to match your language of your file or template.

What languages can I translate to?

The following languages are supported by Translate: English, Filipino, Finnish, German, Greek, Gujarati, Haitian Creole, Hindi, Hungarian, Indonesian, Italian, Japanese, Kannada, Kazakh, Korean, Macedonian, Malay, Malayalam, Norwegian, Polish, Portuguese, Punjabi, Romanian, Russian, Serbian, Slovak, Slovenian, Spanish, Swedish, Tamil, Telugu, Thai, Turkish, Ukrainian, Vietnamese, and Welsh.

Is there any limit on the amount of languages I am able to translate into at once?

Yes, the present limit for languages translation is 20 per translation.

When translating, does one have a maximum number of character limit?

Yes, each translation action is currently limited to 30K characters. If you cross the threshold, consider translating lesser characters.

Will the translation affect the font used in my text?

The target language's default font is automatically selected. You can alter the font using the Text pane's font picker or by using font recommendations.

WORKING WITH LAYERS

Discover how to use Adobe Express to open, reorganize, group, ungroup, & lock layers.

Layers serve as layers on your canvas in which you can effortlessly position shapes, videos, and other elements of design. With layers, you can easily reposition individual components inside your design and create visual hierarchy.

Learn layer basics

Open the layer pane

Layers are arranged in a stack in the layer pane, located to the right of the canvas. Select the Layers icon from the toolbar to open the layers pane.

Rearrange layers

You can bring your layer forward / you can send backward via choosing your layer & moving it upward or downward. This will adjust position for your corresponding object on your design.

Hint:

You may additionally, rearrange your object order in your canvas. Choose & right-click any object then select from any of the four of these: **Bring To Front, Send Backwards, Bring Forward, / Send To Back.**

Group & ungroup objects in designs

To group your objects in design:

1. Press down your shift key and choose the objects of your choice to group within your design.
2. Choose **Group** on your left pane or employ **Cmd+G** (on Mac) or **Ctrl+G** (on Windows).

To ungroup any layer, choose your grouped layer in your stack and tap **Ungroup** on your left pane.

Lock layers

You can lock a layer to avoid the objects getting easily moved on the canvas.

1. Choose any layer from your layer pane.
2. Tap on the **Lock** icon on your left pane.

Note:

- While employing Adobe Express on a desktop computer, you could add up to 200 layers; on a mobile device, you could addup to 50 layers.
- Once a layer is locked, its order cannot be changed in the layer pane.

USING CHATGPT TO EXPLORE THE ADOBE EXPRESS TEMPLATES

Engage with Adobe Express's GPT to browse & access templates that are customized to your requirements

Make use of Adobe Express GPT for exploring Adobe's Express templates directly within ChatGPT that are most suited to your needs.

Explore templates

1. Sign into your **Adobe Express GPT** using your own ChatGPT Plus account.

2. In your message field, give a description of what you would like to create.

   For instance: Make a badge for my chocolate shop.

3. Choose any template from your suggestions. This will open your template in your Adobe Express's editor.

4. Then customize your template via adding text, design elements, images, and more. Log in to your Adobe's Express to share or download your design.

Important:

- At present, ChatGPT Plus, Teams, & Enterprise users are the only ones with access to Adobe Express GPT.
- You need to be signed in via your Adobe ID in order to access and modify Premium templates within your Adobe's Express editor.

Chatting with the Adobe Express GPT

Enter in a prompt to specify what you would like to generate while using Adobe Express's GPT. Here are some examples to get you motivated:

- Create a brand identity for my downtown Seattle coffee shop.
- Make a poster for my high school's next soccer tournament.
- Create a flyer to promote my restaurant's big opening.

PRESENTATION

Importing PowerPoint file

You can Import PowerPoint file & modify it within your Express by inserting images, text, animations, and even more.

1. In your Express homepage, choose **Start from your content** within your **For you** unit.
2. Then upload any PowerPoint presentation on your device.
3. Choose **Open** in your **Import** window to access your presentation in your Express editor.

Important:

- PowerPoint Import is restricted to a the maximum of one hundred(100) pages.
- While importing any PowerPoint presentation, presenter notes, animations, audio, and video will not be imported.
- Your file is converted Audio, video, animations, and presenter notes will not be imported when importing a PowerPoint presentation.
- Your file is converted automatically & saved as an Express file within **Your stuff**.

Result

Your imported template opens within your Express editor. The template can be customized via the addition of pages using different templates, as well as by including text, graphics, animations, and other objects.

Explore presentation templates

You can design your presentation with the high-quality presentation templates accessible in the Adobe Express.

1. In your Express homepage, you should hover over the **Presentation** within your **For You** section.
2. Choose the Browse templates.

choose "Browse templates" for exploring your presentations templates which are accessible on Adobe Express.
3. Go through your presentation templates or choose for narrowing down your outcomes.
4. Then select your template.

Result

Your selected template opens within your Express editor. The template can be customized via the addition of pages using different templates, as well as by including text, graphics, animations, and other objects.

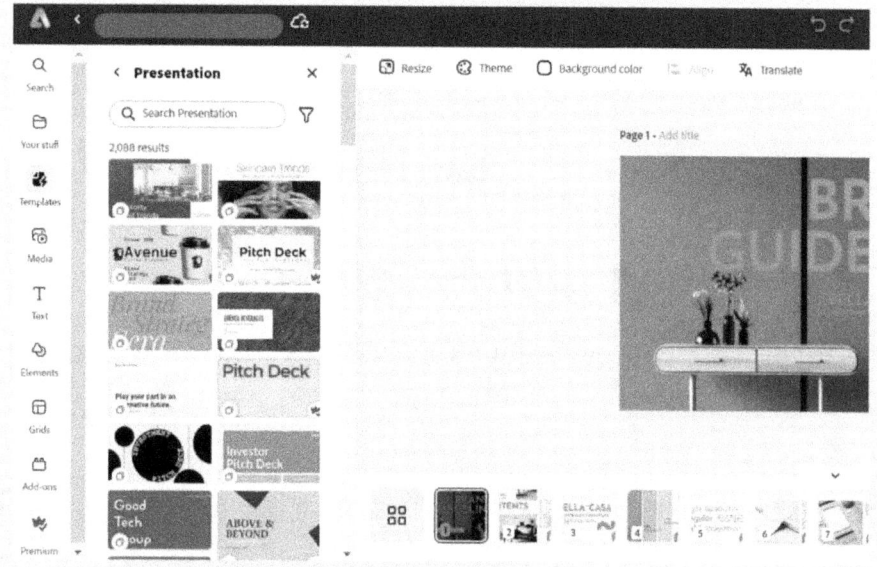

Presentation template library

Manage pages

You can use your page management toolbar on your Express to manage your presentation pages.

Your page management tab in Adobe Express can be used to help arrange, insert, delete, & duplicate pages while working on your presentation slides.

Before you start:

You should import PowerPoint presentation or look through expertly designed presentations templates to get inspiration and then modify them to suit your requirements.

Action	Description
Reorder pages	Drag and reorder the pages to change the order in which the slide appears in your presentation.
Insert, delete, or duplicate pages	Hover over a page and select the **page actions** icon to insert, delete, or duplicate a page. You can also select a page and press **Delete** on your keyboard to delete a page.
View all pages	Select the **View all pages** icon in the page management bar to view all the slides together.

Presenting your design

Discover how to use Adobe's Express presentation documents to create full-screen presentations.

1. Open your Express homepage and choose **Document >** then **Presentation**.
2. Scroll through your available presentation templates.
3. Choose one template and modify as needed.
4. Tap on **Present** in your editor's menu bar.
5. Choose **Present from the first slide/Present from the current slide**.

Result

The **Present from first slide & Present from current slide**, will result in full-screen presentation acquaintance. With your mouse or your keyboard, you can navigate through your presentation and then press escape when you want to exit your presentation.

Important:

- It is not possible to use full screen presentation for your presentation document that were generated prior to March 15, 2024, when the feature was released. But, by creating a fresh presentation, you may still present them

on full screen mode. Include the previous presentation's pages in the current one. Under **Your Stuff**, you can view previous presentation documents.
- Presently, hyperlink is not supported on full-screens presentation mode.

BACKGROUNDS

Adding background image on your design

You can add fascinating background images on your designs easily.

1. Go to your **Adobe's Express homepage** and select the desired design to work with.
2. To select a background image which goes well with your design, choose **Upload from device**.
3. To make it your background image, use your **Set as page backgrounds** option from your image pane.
4. Press **Download**.

Hint:

If you want to remove your newly inserted background, choose your **Detach Page Background** option!

Removing background from your video

You can remove your background from your videos using the Express background features, helps in creating stunning visuals.

1. Open your **Express homepage** then select the design which you want to work on.

2. To open your media section, navigate to your left pane & the choose **Media** > then tap **Videos**.

3. Choose the **Upload from devices** to insert video into your design on which you would like to remove it background.

4. Then choose the **Remove background** in your **Video pane**.

5. Then tap **Download**.

Hint:

Opt for getting back your background with your icon when you desire to retain your existing background photo.

Replacing page backgrounds from images

You can easily replace your page backgrounds on your designs. Enhance your creativity & make adjustments to your designs like a Pro.

1. launch your **Adobe Express's homepage** then open the design you would like to work on.

2. From your left pane, choose **Media** > then tap **Photos**.

3. Choose **Upload from devices** to insert an image into your page.

4. Choose the image then choose the **Replace background** in your **Image pane**.

5. Then tap on **Download**.

Hint:

You may swiftly set a photo as your background via selecting the **Set as page background** while no photo is presently applied on your design.

GENERATIVE AI

Generating images from text with generative AI

Adobe Express's **Text to Image** features allows you to create amazing images from simply a description.

Use Adobe Express's **Text to Image** function to make your idea a reality. Give your image a description, and watch generative AI work its magic. For quick and enjoyable results, employ **Text to image** within your **Quick Actions** option. Alternatively, make use of the capability in your editor when incorporating another design on Adobe Express.

Generate extraordinary images for your designs using Text to image

Make use of **Text to im**ages for instantly creating fun, professional-quality photos in fashionable styles, which include product photos, cyberpunk, digital art, and more. See how to use Adobe Express's

Text to image artificial intelligence (AI) feature to create images for your Facebook post.

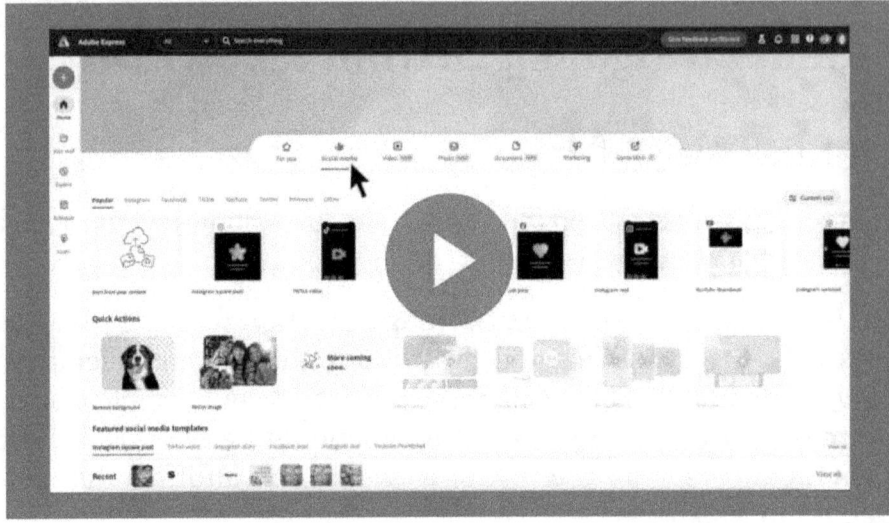

1. On your Adobe's Express homepage, from your **Get Started**, hover over your **Facebook post** and choose the **Create from scratch**.

2. Once your editor opens, from within your **Media** pane, choose the **Text to image** then select your Image size of your post.

3. Explain what you would like to generate in specifics and choose **Content type**.

4. Select one or as much you want from Style options then choose **Generate** to see your astonishing image and comparable **Results**.

5. Personalize your design with your Adobe Stock images, design assets, text, and more.

6. Then **Download** design to your device or choose **Share** to circulate to your social media handles.

Generating text effects with generative AI

With Adobe Express, you can apply a distinct style & texture to generate amazing text effects with just a description.

Use the **Text effects** tool in the editor to include the feature into another Adobe Express design, or use it in your **Quick actions** option on your homepage for quick and enjoyable results.

Using text effects to add impact to your designs.

Create visually striking headlines for your designs, which includes promotional materials, your social media content, and more, by creating high-quality textures and effects for your text. See how to use Adobe Express to add eye-catching flyers and high-quality texts effects.

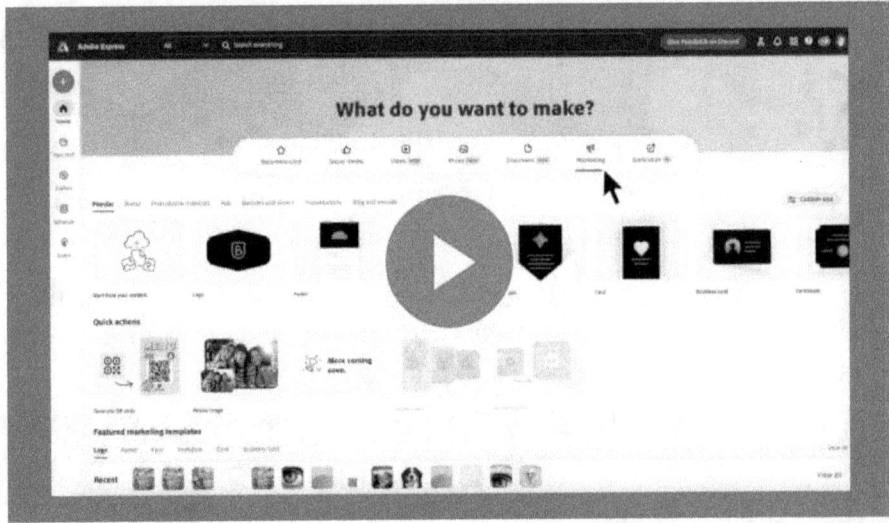

1. In your Adobe Express homepage, under the **Get started**, you should hover over the Flyer and choose **Create from scratch / Browse Templates**.

2. On your editor, choose the **Upload from devices** to upload media or you look through your Adobe Stock images and videos. Personalize your flyer with shapes, audio tracks, icons and more.

3. Insert text effects in your headline to make it outstanding. Then choose **Text** on your left pane then choose the Add your texts.

4. Choose the **Text effects** on your text pane. Describe what effect you would like to make or you choose from your **Sample effects**. Select your preferred **Font** and how you'd like to fill your text.

5. Tap on **Generate** to see your text effect & similar **Results**.

6. Then choose **Download/Share**.

What comes next?

Using AI-powered features & advice which eliminate guesswork, you can create designs more quickly and easily. Discover how to use generative AI to create image from text.

Inserting or replacing objects using your Generative fill

Use Adobe Express's Generative Fill feature to rethink what's possible. By applying simple text input; you may quickly and easily add or replace elements from an image and obtain results of excellent quality.

Insert or replace objects

1. In your Adobe Express homepage, hover over whatever you desire to create then choose the **Create from scratch**.

2. Choose Upload from device or you look through your Adobe Stock images to add your image into your file.

3. Then choose an in your file in order to open your **Image** pane and then you select the **Generative fill**.

4. Adjust your **Brush size** slider to specify your preferred brush size.

5. Make use of your brush to highlight an area or object in your image.

6. In your prompt box, you should describe changes you would like to see the choose **Generate**.

7. Then select a photo from your generated results.

8. Then you **Download** the photo into your device / **share** it among your audience online.

Hint:

- When you are unhappy with your generated results, all edits can easily be undone, and your image can be reverted back into it original state by employing your **Restore image** ↺ symbol within your **Generative fill** pane.
- You may remove objects from an image on the exact workflow whenever you are inserting or you replacing objects on that image.

Removing objects from your image with the Generative fill

Remove objects off an image quickly and easily! Generative fill makes it simple to remove unwanted elements from your image, highlighting its designated focal point & generating stunning images.

Removing objects from your image

1. Open your image in the Adobe's Express editor.
2. Then tap on the image to open your Image pane and then choose **Generative fill.**
3. Make use of your **Brush** slider for selecting the brush size.
4. Then brush the undesirable object from your image.
5. Leave your prompt box empty, then choose **Generate**, and select an image in your generated results.
6. Then **Download** the image to your device / **Share** it among your audience online.

Generate editable templates using Text to Template

You can generate your editable templates for your social posts, flyers, posters, & cards from just your text description in seconds.

Create customizable templates

1. In your Express homepage, tap on **Generative AI**.
2. The scroll to your **Text to Template** sector and type in the description for the template that you would love to generate.
3. Then select **Generate**.
4. Choose your template to access it in your editor and perform further modifications.
5. Choose **Download** to save it on your device, or tap on **Share** to share your design with audience online.

Tips to make your ideas come to life

- **Describe the topic or event for which you are generating your template**: for instance, Indicate if it's an advertisement for a forthcoming occasion.

- **Try various variations for a template**: To see comparable designs and choose your favorite, select See variations from your template's header.
- **Begin from any template & make it your own**: After choosing your template design, use the editor to customize it including text effects, modifying the fonts, changing the backdrop, and more.

CREATING AND MANAGING BRANDS

Creating brand in Adobe Express

With Adobe Express, you can quickly and easily generate consistent branded contents.

Establish your brand within the Adobe Express, comprising logos, colours, and fonts, to make it simple to include brand assets into any kind of design.

Creating your brand

Important:

You need to be logged into Adobe Express Premium version in order to create any brand.

1. In your Express homepage, choose **Brands** > then tap **Create brand**.
2. Then create your brand name.

3. Once you have created your brand folder, you should insert in any brand component: upload **Logos**, choose **Colours**, select **Fonts** from your Adobe Fonts library, & then upload graphics.

What comes next?

By promoting your brand to others, you may empower your team to generate consistent branded contents.

Managing shared brands in Express

Use shared brand kits to create branded content that is consistent throughout the team and manage your shared brands on Adobe Express.

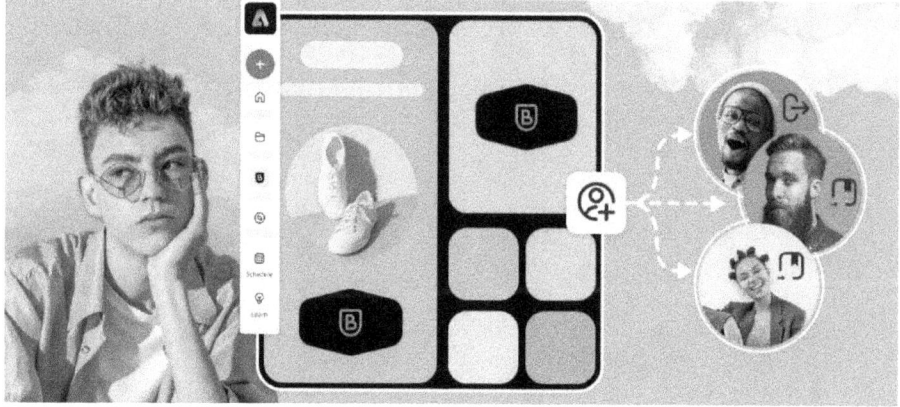

Share a brand

1. In your Express homepage, navigate to **Brands**.
2. From **Brands**, choose the brand which you would prefer to share.
3. Choose **Invite people** on your top right & type in the name / email address for the person you want to share your brand with.

Getting started to access the shared brands

- **Email**: Look for an invitation to use shared brand in your inbox.
- **In-apps notification center**: Locate the bell icon in the top right corner of your screen to see when you received an invite. then Accept Invite.

Hint:

Navigate to your **Brands** section to access a shared brand with you. Your shared brands can be identified with one another by looking for any shared icon & tag beneath your brand name.

Leaving shared brand with you

1. In your Adobes Express homepage, navigate to **Brands**.
2. Hover your mouse over your shared brand & choose the 3 dots.
3. Choose **Leave**.

ADDING CUSTOM FONTS

You may quickly and simply manage brand & style guidelines by adding your fonts to Adobe Express via the web.

The Adobe's Custom Font lets you to tweak your brand variables, adapt your character compositions, & effortlessly embody your peculiar identity & values. Adobe Express allows you to import your own font & add it on your font picker.

Adding customs fonts to your Brand on Adobe Express

1. In your Express homepage, choose **Brands**.
2. Then select any **Brand** to put in custom fonts.
3. Tap on **Add your fonts** > then select **Upload**.
4. In your pops-up window, choose Add **fonts**. Then search for any font in your device then tap **Add**.

Adding your custom fonts into your file on Adobe Express

1. You should start with any file in your Adobe Express homepage. In your editor, choose **Text** > then tap on **Add your text**.

2. On your **Text** pane, open your fonts drop-down & tap on **Upload**.

3. From your pop-up window, choose **Add fonts**. Then search for any font in your device then tap **Add**.

4. To make use of your font, choose your own font from the list of **uploaded fonts** by going to your **Text** pane's fonts dropdown menu.

- **For users of Enterprise**
  You need to be registered for a purchased enterprise account in order to utilize custom fonts. The enterprise account administrator can grant you permission to use a custom font upon request, which you can then download via your Administrator Console.

Supported font files

The Adobe's Express supports the .otf & .ttf font files which are below 512 Mb.

Your usage with your Adobe's Fonts Service & uploading of your custom fonts are governed through the Adobe's General Terms of Use. It is your responsibility to confirm that you possess the appropriate licenses and rights in order to use & upload your fonts to Adobe Express Services. Adobe has the right to deactivate a font you uploaded, and replace it with a different font, or terminate your account if it is found that you don't have the necessary authorizations and rights to use the uploaded font.

Please be aware that the design and appearance of your Express contents may change when we replace the font you uploaded with a different font.

Commonly asked questions

After my express membership expires, what will happen to the fonts?

Your custom fonts that you've uploaded will stay as a component of your brand even after your membership gets expired. You're going to be capable of opening existing files which employ a custom font, nevertheless, your text is going to remain in read-only state. You may manually alter your font into one that's free for editing your text.

If my brand is deleted, what will happen to the fonts?

When you delete a brand, it doesn't delete your uploaded font connected to that brand. In your brand manager, you can choose to delete a particular font by selecting your trash symbol next to its name.

I get a message saying that my brand-named file is locked when I attempt to open it. HOW can I Access MY FILE?

When your membership gets expired, you may open existing files that make use of any custom font. The text will only be available for read only state, though. You may manually alter your font to one that's free for editing your text.

How do I use a shared brand with a restricted font?

When you accept any shared brand which consists of any custom font, you have to upload your licensed copy for that font in order to utilize the brand.

1. You should go to Adobe Express from any of your desktop browser.
2. Access any of your existing file or make a file.
3. Choose your Brand switcher on your right rail & choose the Brand which you want to use.
4. You'll then be prompted to upload the custom font to use that Brand in your projects.
5. Choose your font file you want to upload on your desktop.

    You are ready to use the Brand on your Adobe's Express files on your mobile phone and across the web.

If I have an education account, how can i access the custom fonts?

The education account administrator must upload your custom fonts in order to use them. The education account user will be able to use the fonts on a project after they are uploaded.

Is it possible for me to coedit a file with a font that another user uploaded?

Only after uploading your font to your font picker you may co-edit any file using a font that was provided by another user. To add a font from another user to your font picker, you must have a premium account.

CREATING AND SHARING CREATIVE CLOUD LIBRARIES

Retain your design assets in a place, and effortlessly make consistent content together with your team with the Adobe Express.

Create Libraries

1. In your homepage, choose **Your stuff** in your left pane, & then choose **Libraries** > then tap **Create library**.

2. Then name your library on your pop-up box then choose **Create**.

3. Combine every one of your assets via adding **Colours**, **Graphics**, and **Fonts** on your library.

Hint:

By pressing the three dots ••• icon, you may quickly handle tasks within your library like **Rename, Use as brand, Delete** and even more.

Share Libraries

1. You should tap on your **Share** icon > then select **Invite people**.
2. Type in an email address. Then make use of your dropdown list to specify your editing permission either to **Can edit / Can view**.
3. Then tap on **Invite to edit / Invite to view**, all based on your permission settings.

Accepting invite to Libraries

1. You should accept library notification in your email / from your in-apps notification center.
2. Navigate to **Your stuff** > the select **Libraries**, to access your shared library.

What comes next?

To ensure consistent branding across all designs, use your Adobe Express to get rid of any inconsistent fonts, colours, or graphics.

LOCKING AND UNLOCKING ELEMENTS IN YOUR DESIGNS

Discover how to keep certain elements of a design locked in order to retain a consistent style.

By locking elements, teams may generate on-brand content more quickly. It makes the editing experience easier for others via locking elements which ought not to be changed or enabling certain modifications using more locking options.

Lock & unlock your text

1. Open design on your Express editor, then choose the text you'd like to **lock / unlock**.

2. In your left pane, tap on your **Lock** 🔒 icon to lock & your **Unlock** 🔓 icons to unlock.

3. You may optionally choose your checkbox beside the **Text can be replaced** on your Lock setting pane.

   Please note:
   - Whenever you select your checkbox, your text will be editable while making sure the position stays intact and with on altering of its size, colour, animations or font.
   - This feature is accessible on the Team, Premium, & Enterprise plans.

Locking and unlocking images

1. Open design on your Express editor, then choose the text you'd like to lock / unlock.

2. In your left pane, tap on your **Lock** 🔒 icon to lock & your **Unlock** 🔓 icons to unlock

3. You may optionally choose your checkbox beside the **Image can be replaced** on your **Lock setting** pane.

   Take note:
   - Whenever you select your checkbox, image will be replaceable or reframed with no altering of it styling attributes, like animations, adjustments, and effects.
   - This feature is accessible on the Team, Premium, & Enterprise plans.

Important:

- **Locked text**: Text that employs non-default layout preference (such dynamic & circular) cannot have lock settings applied to it. These text items may only be completely locked or unlocked.

- **Locked images**: The background is lost when photos are replaced out. Before replacing your photos, if necessary, your background must be removed.

What comes next?

Discover how to configure template brand style controls.

SET BRAND STYLE CONTROLS ON TEMPLATES

Find out how to add controls for brand style into the templates that you wish to share.

Use your styles control settings to limit the team's access to only approved fonts and colours in order to maintain brand consistency. Once you activate **style restrictions** in a template, contributors are unable to modify these settings and can only access the colours and fonts within your **Brands / Library** where the template is stored.

Style restrictions

The Style restrictions are exclusive to Teams & Enterprise subscriptions. Make sure you set up a brand kit that includes fonts and colours before turning on the restrictions. Users are unable to access the **Themes** pane and apply colours onto the template after the font and colour restrictions are enabled. In addition, **Text lockups & Text effects** are going to be disabled in order to avoid applying a style which might be off-brand for the template.

Few exemptions to brand colours & font enforcement:

Colour

- The collaborators will still be able to access true white, true black & transparent options from your colour pickers.
- The copying & pasting of your content will eliminate styling & default into a neutral colour from your brand / library.

Font

- When a collaborator uses the **Translate** tool in a template that has font restrictions, accurate translation may need fonts other than those in your **brand / library** on the generated pages.

- Users can access a font that was not included in your brand / library when the template was published in their remixed versions.

- Copying & pasting your content is going to remove styling as well as default into neutral font from your brand and library.

Sharing template with controlled permissions

1. Once your design is set to be saved, tap on your **Share** button.
2. On your Make a template tab, choose **Adding to Brand/Library.**
3. Tap on **Next**.
4. Enter any name for template, and from your **Optional Settings**, choose **Add a note** to enter tips & guidance for your collaborator on how the template is use.
5. Choose any of your existing **Brand / Library**, or you create a fresh one via clicking on the **Add brand icon** / on **Add library** icon.
6. Then tap on **Style restrictions** to specify additional colours & font permissions.
7. Then slide your toggle control for that features which you would like to restrict access to.
    - The colour restricts your access to colours that your brand offers in addition to transparent, white, and black.

- The Font restricts your access to all fonts used in your template and those available within your brand.
8. Tap **Save Template**.

Important:

- Users who do not have a paid Teams, Premium, or Enterprise subscription will see a watermark on templates containing premium content.

- You need to belong to a paid Premium, Enterprise or Teams subscription in order to use or modify custom fonts.

What comes next?

Find out how to use shared templates for creation with collaborators.

Create from shared template

Discover how to use a shared template and make modifications to it.

Certain elements on your shared template or in the editor might have already been restricted by a team member when you are invited to it. You can update your content while maintaining its position & using your shared brand font & colour, depending on the amount of access that has been granted.

Before you start:

You are going to receive an invitation to template, then you have to accept the invite in order to get access to it. You may see your invite within your email / your **Notifications** on your homepage. Locate your brand / library then you tap on **Accept**.

1. On your Express homepage, go to **Brands / Library** within **Your Stuff** and then browse & choose your preferred template.

2. Then choose the Start **a new file**.

3. You may customize your assets in your template via selecting your editable layers.

4. Choose **Download / Share**.

Note:

- When the templates which are shared with you are missing the complete set of colours & Adobe Fonts, your template may possess controls to retain your team on brand. Get across to the person who shared that template and request for additional access.

- When a user Premium creates a template employing free assets in Adobe Express, individuals on the Free plan are able to use it just like it is. Nevertheless, when the user Premium makes use of premium content, the receiver will observe a watermark.

- To utilize custom fonts, Free users must upgrade as custom fonts are a premium feature.

CONTENT SCHEDULER

Overview of Content Scheduler

You can plan, schedule, preview, & publish your content with just click across several social media networks using your Content Scheduler in Adobe Express.

With just one click, you can plan, schedule, preview, & publish across every of your social media platforms using Adobe Express's Content Scheduler, saving you time.

Plan: This Plan your themes, campaigns or topics through drafting & ideation tools.

Preview: This allows you to preview how your post will appear like once it's published, helps build your confidence as to what you post.

Schedule: This set content to appear at the precise appropriate time, to make sure that your content gets to the most viewers as feasible.

Publish: This helps to save time via publishing your Instagram, X (Twitter), Pinterest, LinkedIn, Facebook, & TikTok posts with just one click.

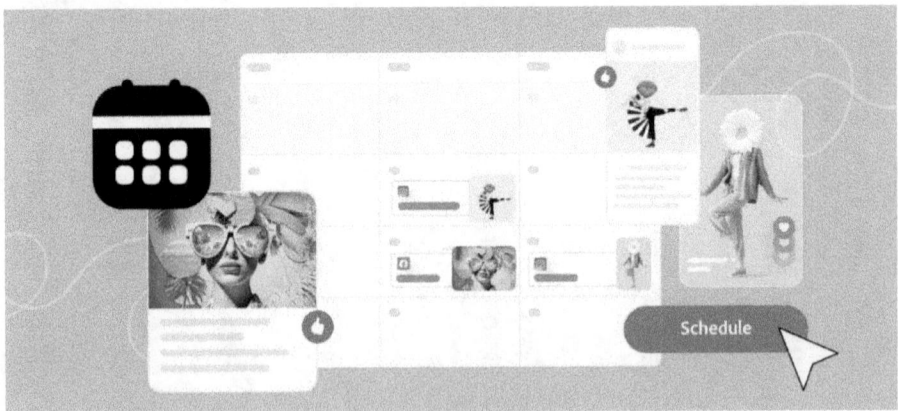

For Content Scheduler to work, which subscription is required?

The **Schedule** 📅 is not presently accessible to users which access the Adobe Express through a K-12 school and district school.

Important:

Enterprise users can access **Schedule** 📅 unless your IT admin restricts access.

What is the function of Content Scheduler?

Connecting your social media accounts

You can link the Contents Scheduler to your Facebook, Instagram, X (Twitter), LinkedIn, Pinterest, & TikTok accounts.

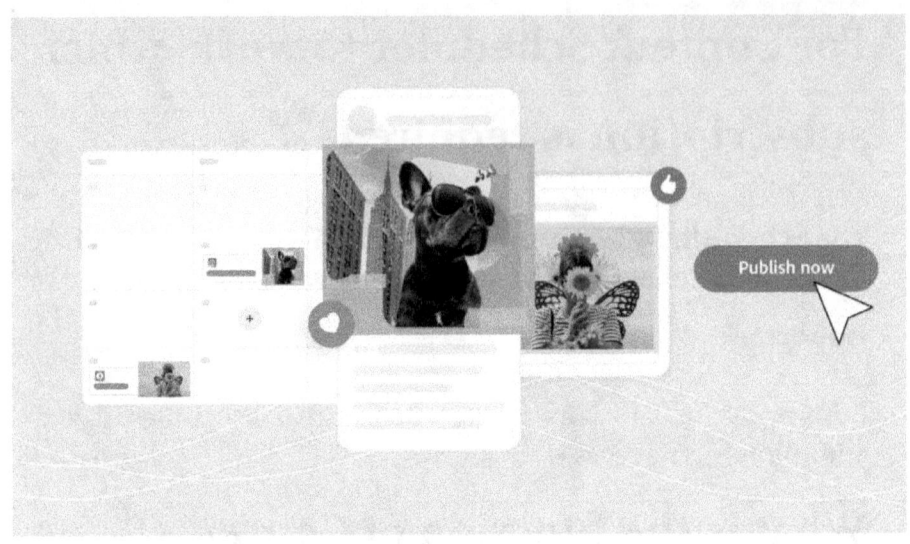

Scheduling your social media posts

Set up your posts for publishing at a particular date & time across social networks.

Tip:

You may configure your calendar perceptions by either week or month. Choose **Schedule** from your left pane. To choose your preferred setting, go to your homepage and tap on **Week / Month** at the top of your calendar.

Connecting your social accounts

Before scheduling posts, connect your social media account to your Adobe's Express Content Scheduler.

Connecting your social accounts to your Content Scheduler

The Adobe's Express Contents Scheduler can be connected to accounts on Facebook, Instagram, LinkedIn, Pinterest, X (Twitter), and TikTok.

Important:

To connect with a page, profile, or group, you must be its admin.

Connect Facebook

1. Tap on **Schedule** 🗓 on your Express menu in your homepage.

2. Tap on **Manage connections** and then select **Connect** beside your Facebook logo.

3. Tap on **Continue** and type in your Facebook log-in credentials on your dialogue box.

4. Choose all Facebook pages which you are an admin and tap **Next**.

5. Allow access permissions for your Adobe Express & tap **Done**. To ensure the correct functioning of Adobe Express, turn on every option.

6. Choose the page/profile which you would like to connect on your Adobe Express in your dropdown. Then tap Connect.

7. Then once you get confirmation, stating that your account is now connected, tap the Return to **Adobe Express**.

Connecting your Instagram through Facebook account

Use Content Scheduler to schedule posts by connecting your Instagram account. Additionally, you may convert your Instagram account's status to "business." Visit to https://help.instagram.com/502981923235522 to find out how to change your account on Instagram into business account. Make sure the relevant Facebook Page has been connected to it. Your account can be upgraded for free.

1. Choose Schedule 📅 on your Express menu on your homepage.

2. Then tap on **Manage connections** then choose **Connect** beside to your Instagram logo.

3. Then choose **Connect via Facebook**. You should connect every Instagram profiles on your Facebook page to allow automatic publishing.

4. Make sure you are logged into your right Facebook account, then tap **Continue**.

5. Then select all your Instagram Business accounts that you would like to link to the Adobe Express. Then tap **Next**.

6. Choose all of your Facebook pages that you would like to connect to.

Hint:

Tap on **Select all** for connecting all pages for your comfort. You will be able to choose the right account to use in your next step.

7. Make sure all your permissions are switched to **yes**. Then tap **Done**.

8. Choose the account that you would like to your Adobe's Express Content Scheduler. Once you've received confirmation that your account is connected, select **Return to Adobe Express**.

Connect Pinterest, X (Twitter), LinkedIn, / TikTok

1. You should choose Schedule from your Express menu list to open your calendar.

2. Then choose **Manage connections** then Select your social media website from your list and tap on Connect you would like to link to Adobe's Express.

3. Once redirected to the social media site, type in your log-in details on your dialogue box.

4. Once you get confirmation that your account has been connected, tap on **Return to Adobe Express**.

Commonly Asked Queries

Why do I require business accounts on Instagram?

Instagram posts can only be automatically published to Business accounts. Changing your Instagram account into a business account can help you expand your audience when you post frequently.

Is it possible to publish my Instagram stories using Creator accounts on Instagram?

Stories created using an Instagram Creator's account cannot currently be published on Instagram due to restrictions. We advise switching to a business account type on Instagram if you want to publish stories.

Can I use a Personal account to publish?

At present, personal accounts aren't supported.

Is it possible I publish Stories and Reels on Instagram?

Instagram Reels & Stories can now be published directly to Instagram.

Can I modify the cover photo of my Instagram Reel before it's published?

Yes. An Instagram Reel's cover photo can now be selected by picking frame within your reel prior to publishing. Prior to publishing, choose Edit reel cover > choose a frame for your reel's cover and click Confirm on your Share to social media page.

How can I use Content Scheduler to tag other people on any social media post?

At present, the Content Scheduler does not automatically fill in a user's social media handle when you want to tag them in a post. On Instagram and Twitter, on the other hand, you can manually input the user's handle that you wish to tag in the post's caption; just make sure that you put the @ sign before their username. Then, after the content is published, this tag will function as intended.

Why does Content Scheduler show my social network account as disconnected?

Social media account connections expire every 60 days. To rejoin, choose Schedule > then tap Manage connections, then click Reconnect beside each account in order to reconnect.

Is there a limit on how many posts you can make to social media using Content Scheduler?

With your free plan, you are able to post as many as 1,000 times a month on all six social media platforms (Instagram, Facebook, X (Twitter), LinkedIn, Pinterest, & TikTok).

How much channels will I be able to connect to?

Content Scheduler is improving its posting features for each users as of right now. One account per social media platform (Instagram, Facebook, X (Twitter), Pinterest, TikTok, and LinkedIn,) may be connected by users using the Free package. Consider upgrading into the Premium plan for linking no more than three accounts for each social channel if you want to connect more accounts.

What restrictions apply when publishing content across several social media platforms?

- **Facebook**: allows you to post on three accounts with the exact same message.
- **Instagram**: Three accounts can have the same post made to them.
- **LinkedIn**: Posting the exact same message on three accounts (such as a personal profile AND a company page) is possible.

- **X (Twitter)**: It is prohibited to post the exact same message more than once. Please consult X's spam policy.
- **Pinterest**: Since Pinterest advises revising a post prior to re-sharing, it isn't possible to post the exact same message to several accounts.
- **TikTok**: Since TikTok emphasises content that is original, posting the exact same message to several accounts is not is feasible. If you want to re-share your post, edit your content.

Schedule and publish social media posts

Easily schedule, plan, and preview your content before publishing it to a variety of social media networks.

Manage your own content calendar using Content Scheduler in order to guarantee smooth planning & publishing workflows throughout a variety of social media channels.

Scheduling and publishing social media posts

1. Go to Schedule 🗓 on your Express menus to open your calendar.
2. Tap on **New post**.

3. Using your drop-down option, browse your social media platforms and choose which one you want to connect account to.

   Hint:

   Learn more about each social media channel's media specifications.

4. Choose **Schedule** and type in a date & time on future or in the **Publish now** to instantly publish post.

5. Then add your caption & tap Preview to see how your post will look like.

6. After your post gets ready, choose **Schedule** / **Publish now**.

Media specifications of your social media posts

You should learn more on media specifications of the social media posts on Content Scheduler.

- Facebook
- Instagram
- X (Twitter)
- LinkedIn
- Pinterest
- TikTok

Facebook

Limitations and supported media types to take into account when scheduling any Facebook post:

Characters	55000
Images per post	10
Image size	250 MB The **Schedule** converts the dimensions of the chosen image to 1980px automatically to make it valid for social media networks.
Videos per post	1
Video size	250 MB
Carousel publishing	At this time, not available. Alternatively, you can publish a multi-page post using **Schedule** or post natively to Facebook.

Instagram

(For your Instagram Business & Creator accounts publishing to Feed)

Character limit	2200
Minimum attachments per post	1
Maximum images per post	10 (JPEG or PNG)
Required aspect ratio for images	Must be within a 4:5 to 1.91:1 range
Minimum image width	320
Maximum image width	1440
Image height	Varies depending on image width and aspect ratio
Maximum file size for images	8MB
Maximum videos per post	1 (MOV or MP4)

Video duration	**Maximum:** 60 seconds **Minimum**: 3 seconds
Video size limit	100MB at maximum
Video bitrate	VBR, 5Mbps maximum
Audio bitrate	128kbps
Audio codec	AAC, 48khz sample rate maximum, 1 or 2 channels (mono or stereo)
Video codec	HEVC or H264, progressive scan, closed GOP, 4:2:0 chroma subsampling
Video frame rate	23-60 FPS
Video Picture size	Maximum columns (horizontal pixels): 1920 Minimum aspect ratio [cols / rows]: 4 / 5 Maximum aspect ratio [cols / rows]: 16 / 9

X (Twitter)

Limitations and supported media types to take into account when scheduling any X (Twitter) post:

Characters	280
Images per post	4
Image size	250 MB The **Schedule** converts the dimensions of the chosen image to 1980px automatically to make it valid for social media networks.
Video duration	140s
Video height x width	1024x1028

GIFs per post	1
GIF size	4MB

LinkedIn

Limitations and supported media types to take into account when scheduling any LinkedIn post:

Characters	3000
Images per post	9
Image size	250 MB The **Schedule** converts the dimensions of the chosen image to 1980px automatically to make it valid for social media networks.
Videos per post	1
Video size	1 MB
GIFs per post	1
GIF size	250 frames

Pinterest

Limitations and supported media types to take into account when scheduling any Pinterest post:

Characters	Title: 100 Description: 500
File type	JPEG, PNG, MP4
Media size	20 MB
Media aspect ratio	Pinterest recommends using a 2:3 aspect ratio, or 1000 x 1500 pixels. Pins with an aspect ratio greater than 2:3 may get cut off in people's feeds.

TikTok

Limitations and supported media types to take into account when scheduling any TikTok post:

Caption Characters	2200
File formats	TikTok accepts 1 video in MP4, WebM, or MOV format.
Video duration	**Minimum:** 3 seconds **Maximum:** 3 minutes (180 seconds)
Aspect ratio	1080px x 1920px
Video width	**Minimum width:** 360px **Maximum width:** 4096px

QUICK ACTION

Resizing images with Quick Actions

You can resize any image impeccably to fit all your social media channels with your Adobe Express.

Resize your image to make spectacular designs

Using the **Quick Actions**, you may quickly resize your images and immediately download it into your device, also you can use it on a different Adobe's Express design. Find out how to create a stunning design with your resized image.

1. On your Express homepage, from the **What do you want to make**, choose **Photos**.
2. Then from your **Photo Quick** Actions option, tap on **Resize image**.
3. Look for file from your device.
4. Tap on any option from your **Resize for** dropdown list. Drag your **Images scale** slider as you need to.

5. Then tap **Download**. You may also choose **Open in editor** for further modifications on your image.

What comes next?

With the generative AI technologies, you can generate amazing text effects & photos that elevate your design to an entirely new level. Then you learn how to easily upload it to social media.

Removing background from your image with Quick Action

Using your Adobe Express's Quick Action, remove an image's background and replace it with a new one that includes graphics and other elements.

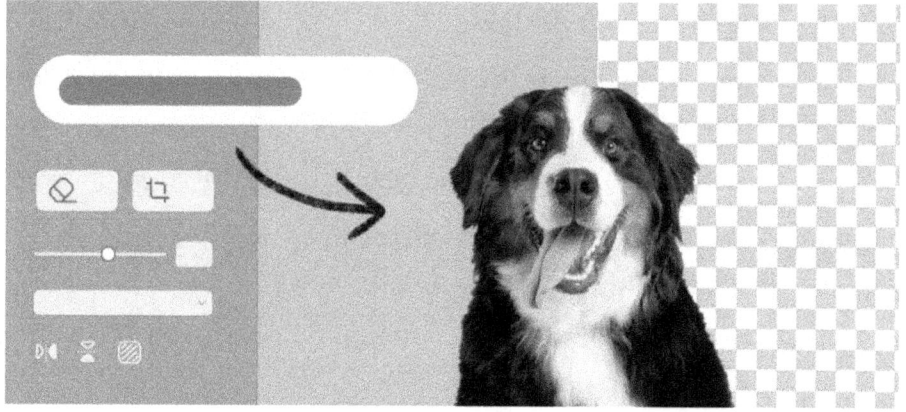

Effortlessly remove your image background in one click

Quick action can be accessed at any stage of your workflow. With a single click, select your photo and remove it background from it. Here's an instance of using Adobe Express to generate a Pinterest concept pin by removing the existing background and adding new one.

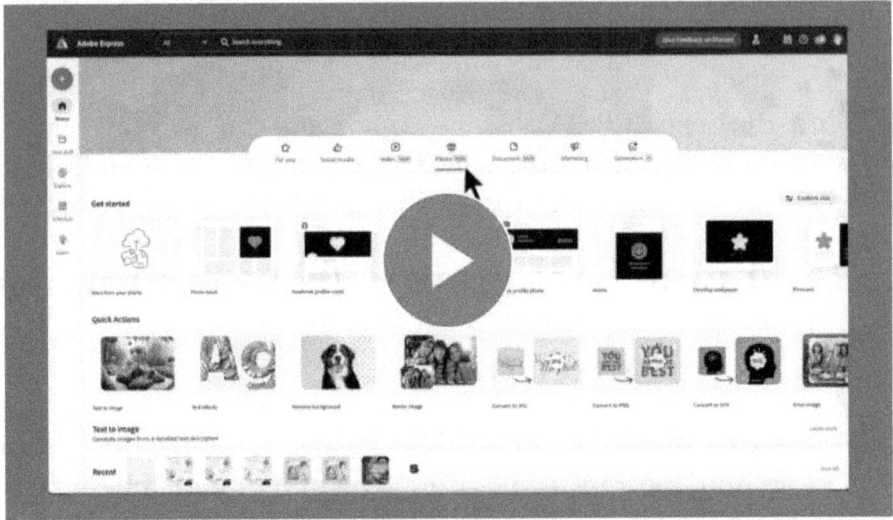

1. On your Express homepage, from the **What do you want to make**, choose **Photos**.

2. Then from your **Photo Quick Actions** option, tap on **Remove background**.

3. Look for file from your device.

4. Then tap **Open in editor** in order to add a fresh background.

5. Then choose **Elements** > then tap **Backgrounds**, to choose your new background photo.

6. Then tap on **Download**.

What comes next?

By using your Library, you can store creatives on the cloud and save time. This improves consistency & real-time collaborations in addition to saving time.

Converting the file formats of your images with the Quick Actions

You can convert your images into other files formats, by making use of quick actions on Adobe Express. Download them for usage on your designs or to share on the internet.

Convert images

1. On your homepage, tap on Photos from **What do you want to make.**

2. Navigate down to your **Photo Quick Actions** sector and then choose the convert images quick action that you want:

    - **Convert to JPG**
    - **Convert to SVG**
    - **Convert to PNG**

3. Search for file from your device.

4. Then tap Download for saving that file in your device or you select **Open in editor** for employing the file in your designs on your Adobe Express.

Supported file formats

JPG

JPG is a particularly appropriate file format whenever size is crucial. Because JPG photos have reduced file sizes, they are perfect for blog posts and social media.

PNG

The PNG conversions keeps all the information on the original file, so the format can be beneficial for complex images when a big file size doesn't seem to be an issue.

SVG

A web-friendly vector's files format called Scalable Vector Graphics (SVG format) allows 2D graphics, illustrations and charts to be scaled upward or downward without compromising image quality. SVG files work well for illustrations, infographics, logos, and more.

What comes next?

Once your file has been successfully converted, add text, sounds, shapes, and other creative elements to your image to bring it to life. To generate a beautiful social media post, open your image in your editor. Then, make use of Schedule for sharing it to the world.

Cropping your image with the Quick Action

You can transform your photos into the perfect size or shape within seconds with the use of **Crop image** Quick Action on Adobe Express.

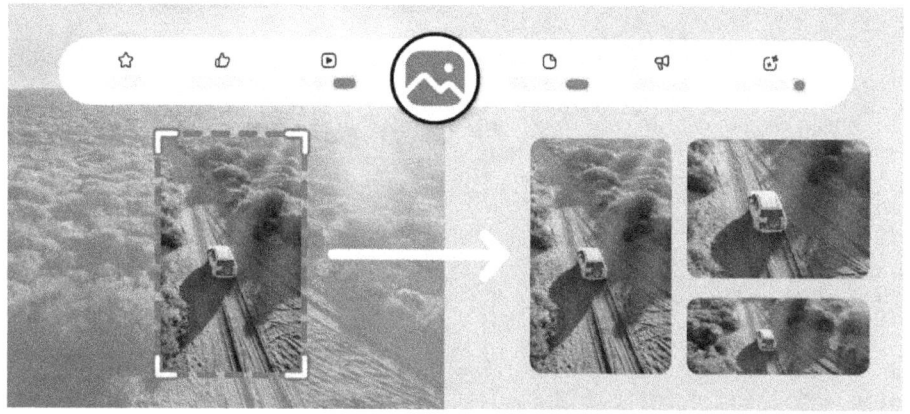

Effortlessly crop your images within seconds

1. On your homepage, from **the What do you want to make**, then tap **Photo**.

2. Navigate down to your **Photo Quick Actions** portion and then tap **Crop image**.

3. Search for any image from your device.

4. The drag on the handles in the corners of your image to make your preferred crop.

5. Then tap Download. You may also choose **Open in editor** to make further modifications on your image.

Animate your character using audio

You can animate any character using your voice with your Adobe's Express quick actions.

Animating characters from audios and incorporate it into your designs

To make an avatar with your voice or an audio file, use the **Animate from audio** quick actions. Get your animated character as a download to share it right away with your audience online or incorporate it into an Adobe Express design. Learn how to use your avatar to make beautiful Facebook stories, Instagram Reels, TikTok videos, & more.

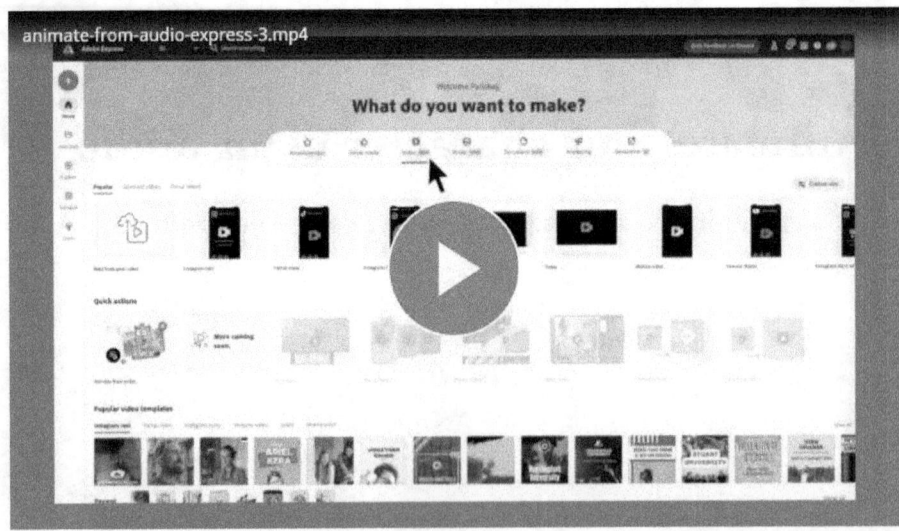

1. On your home page, from the **What do you want to make**, choose **Video**.
2. Scroll down to the **Video Quick Actions** section and select **Animate from audio**.
3. Then tap on **Character** to select your animated character.
4. Then tap on **Background** to select your background image / you choose **Upload image** to select an image on your device.
5. Then tap on **Size**, then use your dropdown option to choose auto-sizing for your social media networks, or select the **Custom** menu to specify your dimensions.
6. Tap on **Record**. Then choose **browse** to insert your audio file in your device rather than making your voice recording.
7. Tap **Download** to save file or you select **Open in editor** in order to employ your animated character as your design with your Adobe Express.

Adding captions on videos with the Quick actions

You can create captions for your videos effortlessly with Adobe Express.

Make use of the feature **of Caption Video** to generate the captions via audio content of your videos. By creating captions for TikTok videos, Instagram Reels, tutorials, educational videos, and other content, you may additionally improve the accessibility of your videos and boost audience engagement.

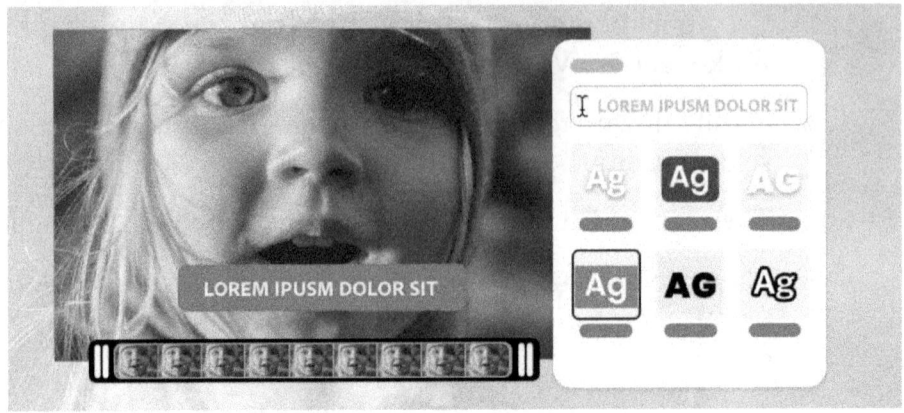

Adding captions

1. On your home page, from the What do you want to make, tap Video.

2. Navigate down to your **Video Quick** actions area and then choose Caption video.

3. Choose your language from your **Language spoken in videos** dropdown.

4. Look for your video file from your device.

5. Employ your **Edit caption text** tab to carry out your changes on your generated caption. Tap on **Choose a style** for animating your caption, or you choose the **Customize colour** to modify your text, shape, / shadow colours.

6. Then Tap **Download**. You may additionally choose **Open in editor** for more edits on your Adobe Express & then **Share** on your social media.

Important:

A video can be uploaded with a maximum duration of five minutes & a file size limit of 1 gigabyte.

Trim your videos with Quick Action

Effortlessly trim videos on the Adobe Express with the Quick Actions.

Trim video to it best length

1. On your home page, from the **What do you want to make**, tap **Video**.

2. Navigate down to your **Video Quick Actions** area and then choose **Trim video**.

3. Then upload any video from device.

4. Then specify your **Start Time & End Time**.

5. Choose any screen **Size** that you prefer.

6. Then tap **Download**. You may additionally choose **Open in editor** for further modifications on your videos.

What comes next?

You can share your videos with your friends using Content Scheduler on Adobe Express.

Resizing your video with Quick Actions

You can resize your videos with your Adobe Express so you can share on all social platform.

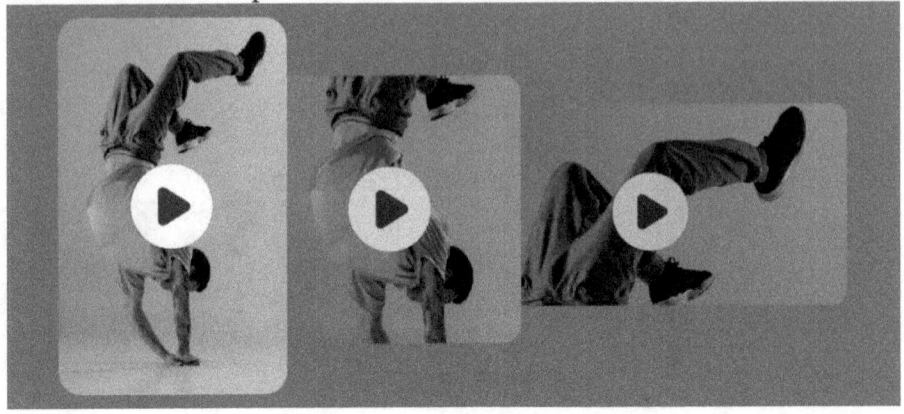

Resizing video for every social media platforms

1. On your homepage, from **What do you want to make**, choose **Video**.

2. Navigate down to your **Video Quick Actions** area and choose **Resize video**.

3. Look through and upload any video in your device.

4. Make use of **Resize for** dropdown option to choose auto-sizing for social media channels, or select your custom selection to specify your dimensions.

5. Choose your orientation & aspect ratio which you would prefer to use, then use your video scale slide to perform your final adjustments.

6. Then tap on **Download**. You may additionally choose **Open in editor** for further modifications on your video.

Hint:

Understand the distinction between your quick actions for Trim video and Resize videos.

The Resize video quick action assists with resizing your video file for your social media channels.

Trim video's quick action cuts down reels to just the necessary information.

Converting video to GIF with Quick Actions

Make use of your Adobe Express in converting your videos to GIFs & share them to social media.

Make memes out of your favourite videos, reaction GIFs, & more. It's simple and quick. To share your content with your internet audience, upload it, choose the quality degree based on wherever you'd like to post it, and share it.

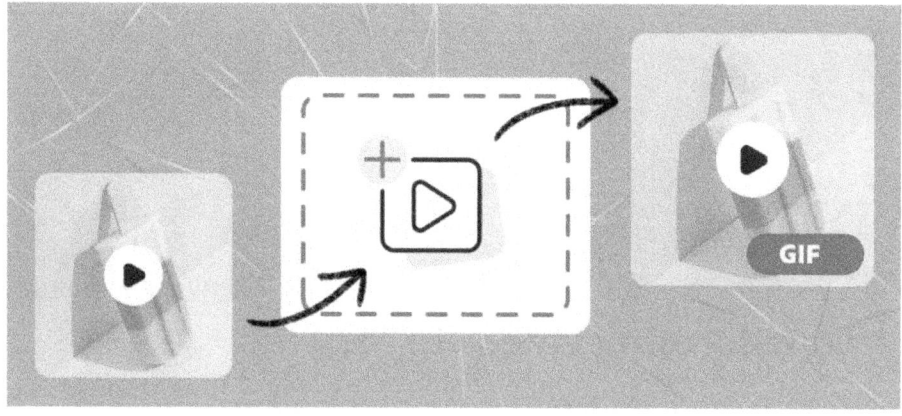

Transforming your videos to appealing GIFs

1. On your homepage, from the **What do you want to make**, choose **Video** > then tap **Convert to GIF**.
2. From device browse & upload your video file.
3. Then drag on the handles in your video's timeline to specify your start & end points.
4. Choose your preferred **File Size**.
5. Choose your aspect ratio from your **Size** dropdown option.
6. Then tap **Download**.

Converting videos into MP4 with Quick Actions

You can convert your videos to an MP4 for seamless sharing with your Adobe Express.

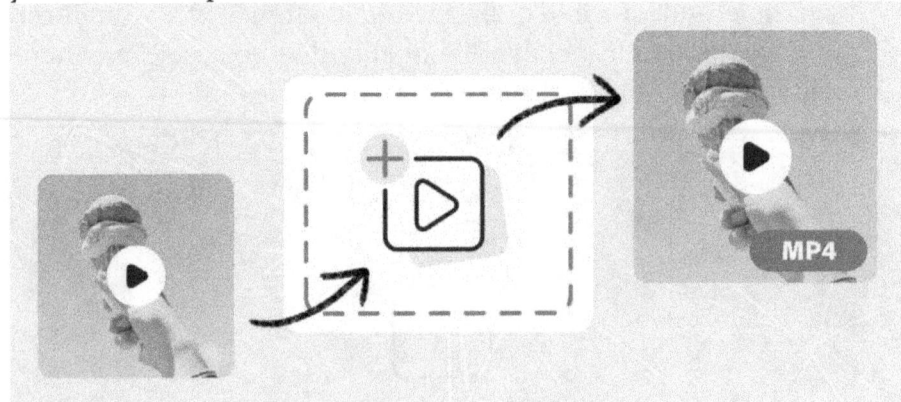

Transforming videos to MP4

1. On your homepage, from the **What do you want to make**, choose **Video**.
2. Navigate down to your **Video Quick Actions** area and choose **Convert to MP4**.

3. Browse and upload a video from your device.

4. Then drag on the handles in your video's timeline to specify your start & end points. tap **Mute** when you would prefer to remove your video original audio.

5. Then tap on **Download**. You may additionally choose **Open in editor** for further modifications on your MP4.

Crop videos within seconds with Quick Actions

You can share a video clip on all social media platform by quickly cropping and adjusting the aspect ratio.

Cropping a video

1. On your homepage from your **What do you want to make,** choose **Video**.

2. Navigate down to your **Video Quick Actions** area and choose **Crop video**.

3. Browse for a video file on your device.

4. Select a pre-set **Aspect ratio** / select **Freeform** to specify your dimensions.

5. Then drag on the handles in your video's timeline to specify your start & end points. tap **Mute** when you would prefer to remove your video original audio.

6. Then tap on **Download**. You may additionally choose **Open in editor** for further modifications on your video.

Merging images and videos with Quick Actions

You can combine videos & images to make a slideshow, compelling video and montages content within seconds.

Merging your Images and videos easily within Adobe Express

1. On your homepage, from **What do you want to make**, choose **Video**.

2. Navigate down to your **Video Quick Actions** area and choose Merge videos.

3. Look for any video or image from your device then tap **Add Media** in order to add more.

4. To trim, mute, duplicate, fit screen, or delete your video or photo, tap on the icons next to your media file.

5. Then tap on **Download**. You may additionally choose **Open in editor** for further modifications on your video.

Converting from or to PDF with Quick Actions

You can convert files from or to PDFs with your Express app to perform in the best form for your teams.

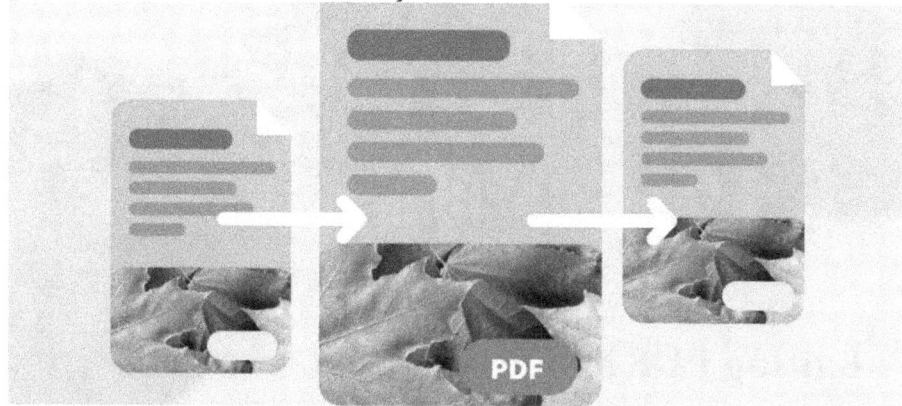

Converting PDFs

1. On your homepage, choose **Document** from **What do you want to make**.

2. On your **Quick Actions** area, tap on your preferred convert PDF quick action:

    - **Convert to PDF**
    - **Convert from PDF**

3. Then upload file in your device.

4. Then tap **Download**.

What comes next?

Integrate your team's comment with edit PDF text & photos quick action.

Editing your PDF images and text with Quick Action

Perform quick edits to your images and text within your PDFs with your Adobe Express.

Editing PDF images and text on Adobe Express

1. In your homepage, from **What do you want to make**, choose **Document**.

2. Navigate down to your **Document Quick Actions** area and tap **Edit PDF**.

3. Look for any PDF from your device.

4. Make use your menu preferences to edit your text & images.

5. Choose your menu options to see your PDF on another formats such as portrait, or you zoom in & out.

6. Then tap **Download**.

Combining files into single PDF with Quick Actions

Make use of Adobe Express app to combine various file formats to one document.

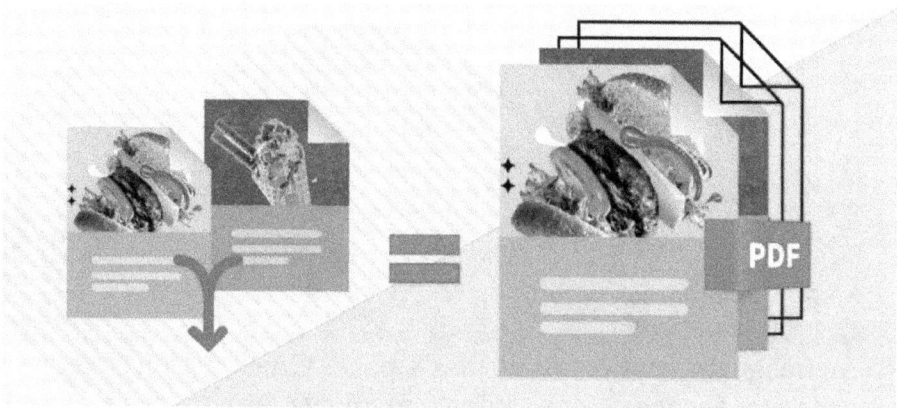

Combine files

Multiple file formats can be combined into single PDF, such as Rich Text Format, Microsoft Excel files, JPGs, even PDFs.

1. On your home page, from the **What do you want to make** > choose **Document**.

2. Navigate down to **your Document Quick Actions** area and choose **Combine files**.

3. Look for files from your device.

4. Choose and drag the pages to reorder or you use rotate ↻ & delete 🗑 icons for rotating and deleting your pages, respectively.

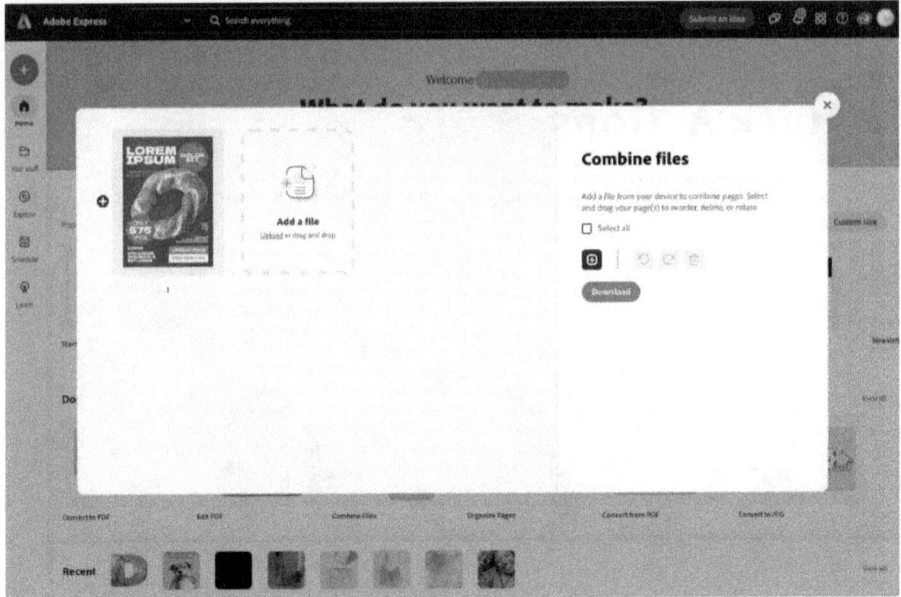

An image displays combine files & pages Quick Actions to combine your files & pages into just one document.

5. Then tap on **Download**.

What comes next?

After combining files, find out how to store your data in cloud docs.

Organizing your Pages into single PDF with Quick Actions

You can make use of your Adobe Express in organizing pages of various file formats within one document.

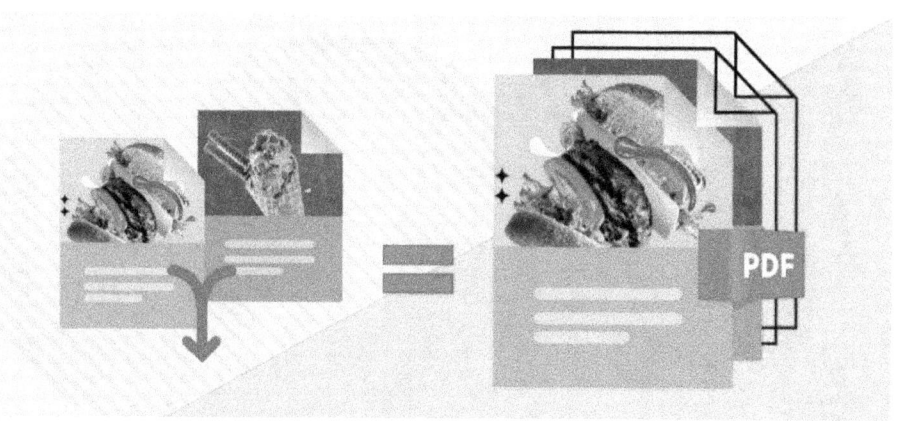

Organize Pages to single PDF

1. On your home page, from the **What do you want to make** > choose **Document**.

2. Navigate down to your **Document Quick Actions** portion and choose **Organize Pages**.

3. Look for files from your device.

4. Reorder your pages, pick and drag them. To reorganize and delete pages as required, use your rotate & delete icons. To add new files, you could additionally use your **Add pages** ⊕ icon

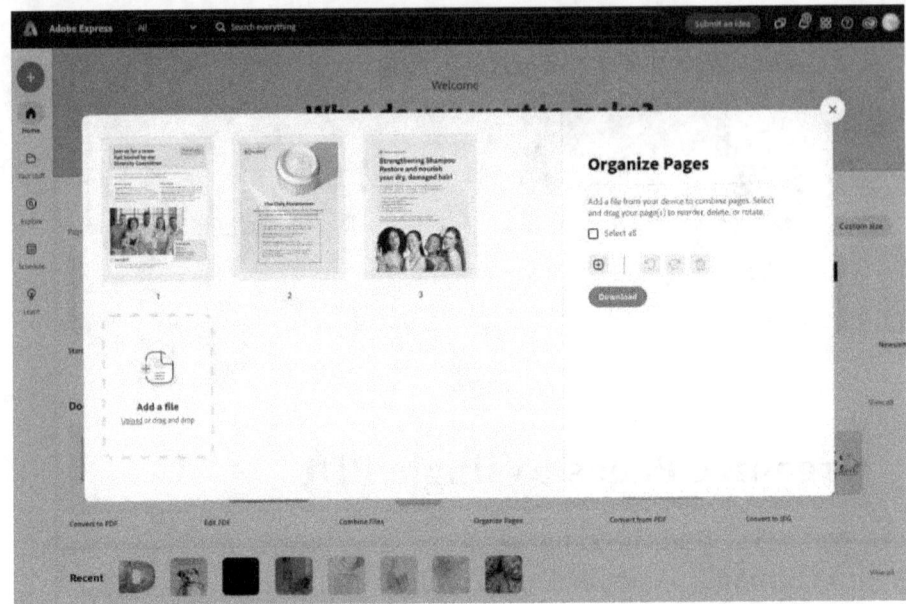

A photo is displaying organize pages Quick Action to modify the sequence and organize pages in document.

5. Tap **Download**.

What comes next?

After combining files, find out how to store your data in cloud documents.

Generating QR code with Quick Actions

In order to improve customer engagement and visibility for your brand, generate your personalized QR codes.

Generating QR codes and using it to customize your designs in Adobe Express

Use the **Generate QR codes** quick action to quickly create QR code, then download it into your smartphone. Use it to create a diversity of designs, such as menus, flyers, banners, business cards, and more. Find out how you can design a standout menu by employing a customized QR code within your Adobe Express.

Generate a QR code

1. In your Adobe's Express homepage, from the **What do you want to make,** choose **Marketing**.
2. Navigate down to your **Marketing Quick Actions** area and choose **Generate QR code**.
3. Then paste your URL of your choice into your box.
4. Customize your QR code by selecting from your from **Style & Colour** options.
5. Choose your **File format** you want to download from the dropdown.
6. Then **Download** the customized QR code into your device.

Using your QR code for designing menu within Adobe Express

1. In your Adobe Express homepage, **under What do you want to make**, select **Document** > then select **Menu** > tap **Create from scratch**.
2. Customize your menu with templates, images, design assets, text, backgrounds, and more.
3. Then tap **Media** > then select **Upload from device**, for uploading the customized QR code.
4. Then tap **Download** or select **Share**, as needed.

What comes next?

You may repurpose your customized QR codes to get different business needs, such as business cards. Make a lasting first impression while networking, with your customized QR code in your business card.

PUBLISH AND SHARE

Collaborate and comment in Adobe Express

Important

There is a desktop version of the latest Adobe Express. Mobile will soon be available.

You can create, brainstorm, and share comments at real-time, all in a single location, employing Adobe Express.

You may quickly invite your team to work together in real time on your designs. To keep yourself organized and collaborate effectively, post comments, tag teammates, and respond to comments all in one location.

Inviting Collaborators to share your files

1. launch a file in your editor, then choose Share > then select **Invite Collaborators** .

2. Type in the name or email address of a team member. You may additionally add a customized message to share an update or provide instructions.
3. configure your editing permission as **Can edit / Can comment** while you **Invite people**.
4. Tap **Invite**.

Place a pin to give context to your comment

1. When you launch a file within your editor, tap on your **Comment** icon in the header.
2. To pin your comment on your page, you should hover across your comment & choose the **Place a pin** 📌 icon. After that, click the page where the pin should be dropped.

   - When a comment is uploaded, your pin appears yellow.
   - Whenever you hover over your relevant comment within your comments pane, the pin becomes blue.

3. Fill out your dialogue box with your comments, then click **Submit**.

Hint: The user name and coloured dot are ideal for teamwork. It enables two users to collaborate in actual time and leave comments to finish a task perfectly.

Tag and notify others of your comments

1. Type the recipient's name / email address after the @ symbol whenever you leave a comment. The names that are available will show up as a drop-down menu when you begin typing.
2. Enter the person's name that you wish to tag.

What comes next?

Learn more regarding privacy & permissions all while you're completing a task!

Host webpage with Adobe Express

Using Adobe Express webpage design essentials, web hosting is easy to do.

You can host your own webpage in preview to real-time mode. Use Adobe Express to share a one-page website without having to sign up for hosting separately.

Host webpage using unique URL

1. When you're ready, finish your webpage & press **Share**.
2. From Publish options, add proper **Credits, Title, & Author Publish** options. If you would like, you can turn off Author.
3. Look for your unique URL by selecting **Share published link**.

Hint:

- To **Republish** an already-existing webpage with updated credits and a title, choose **Share** > then tap **Publish** options.
- Choose **Unpublish** from the **Share** > then tap **Publish options** to publish when your webpage becomes redundant

Commonly asked questions

What's web hosting?

A service called web hosting enables users to publish a webpage or website over the Internet.

What does Adobe Express web hosting entail?

Having your Express file hosted allows you to create an individual URL for every form of content that you publish. Generate distinct links for your pages, videos, and posts. Share this created Link.

Can I use a different server to host content?

Adobe servers host content for Adobe Express. On your own website, you can incorporate hosted content and links to it. The direct hosting of Adobe Express content from your own personal server is not supported.

What is the present maximum number of hosted published Express creations, if any?

At present there aren't any restriction to the amount of published Adobe's Express projects we're going to store for you, therefore continue publishing what you create.

Copying files between your accounts

To copy a file between accounts, share an editable version of such file on Adobe Express.

Copying files among accounts

1. Tap on **Your Stuff** > then select **Files** > then select Yours to **view** every of your files.

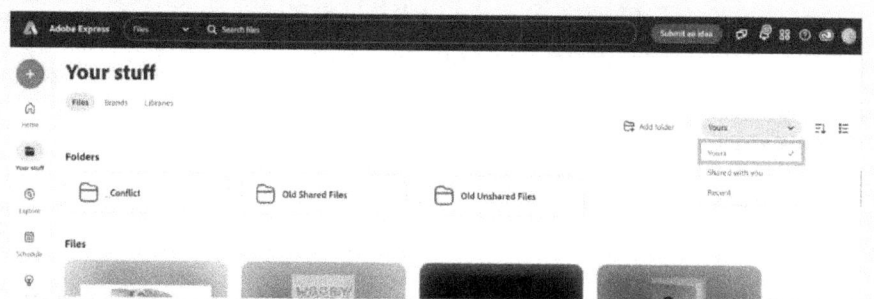

Transfer your file from "**Your stuff**" menu

2. Click **Invite** ⊕ after choosing a file you want to copy.
3. Type in the recipient's email address to send the file.
4. To set your editing permission as **Can edit**, use your dropdown option.
5. Tap on the **Invite**.
6. To access all of the files that were previously shared to them, recipient of that file ought to choose **Your Stuff** > then tap **Files** > then select **Shared with you**.

Get your file from "Shared with you" menu

7. Tap on the file from within your **Shared with you** menu.
8. Then tap Duplicate ⊕.

Important:

- If your file is unbranded, a duplicate copy will be transferred into your account.

- If your files are branded, make an **unbranded copy** to upload to your account.

Caution:

To access files with premium content, you must log in using premium account.

Privacy and permissions

We at Adobe are concerned about your privacy. Here are some specifics regarding projects made with Adobe Express, including who can see them and where to find them.

What will happen and who can view a link that I share?

While sharing any link to your social media, your peers, or integrating a file in a different website, anybody that have URL to your files may view it. Search engines may mention websites and other third-party's social media platforms where you have posted your creations, making your file potentially discoverable by the general public in these situations. If there is sensitive information in your file, think carefully before sharing the URL

Important:

You are the only one who can view your files till you share them.

How can I unpublish a previous shared file from publication?

Making public links currently isn't available on the recently released Adobe Express in desktop web.

When you would like to unpublish any previously published file, you may disable the URL through choosing **Unpublish** in your menu while hovering over your file in **Your stuff**.

Your files won't be transferred automatically if you made use of Adobe Express during 2023 on both desktop, web, and mobile devices. Go to your previous files by choosing Access files from the purple tile under Files, then choose **Unpublish** from the file's options to deactivate the URL.

ADOBE EXPRESS ON MOBILE

Adobe Express for iOS

Create your personal custom designs for your iPad and iPhone by using Adobe Express. Make professional-visually appealing content & share the designs throughout social media.

With your Adobe Express app, you can easily create designs or collages that appear professional by utilizing our collection of assets, which includes images, backgrounds, libraries, videos, or patterns. Additionally, you may select your personal assets from your iPad or phone, import them into your Adobe Express, & quickly generate a design.

Sign in

No Adobe Express application for mobile devices? To get the Adobe Express app, go to your Apple Apps Store.

Getting started with the Adobe Express

1. Press your Adobe Express application icon ⒶA on your iPhone or iPad.
2. Log in using your Google, Facebook, Adobe, or Apple ID.
3. You may start creating, importing, editing, and sharing your graphics, pictures, and videos as soon as you sign in.

Creating designs & collages

With a few simple steps, you may begin creating your very own customize designs.

1. **Start by selecting desired design option.**

   Tap on + icon Ⓐ to begin.

2. Choose any preselected size or custom sizes for your project which is designed to fit your social media, blog posts, print media, and more.

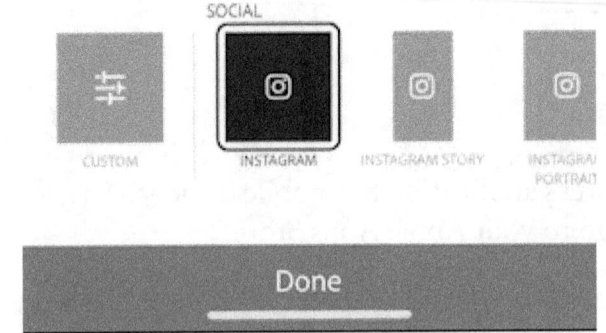

3. Creating your project.

Colours: This select custom colour scheme or choose an app-recommended colour palette.

Animation: This animate your background and your text.

Layout: Picks layout & border width, collage structure, & explore pre-selected themes design.

Brand: This quickly import all your brand assets by just tap.

Resize: Modify your custom size of your project / choose a distinct preselected size selection.

4. Adding pages to your project

   - **Add** - – This makes new pages within your project.
   - **Duplicate** – This replicate your design on new page.
   - **Trash** – This delete pages

5. Edit your project. Tap on the + icon to begin the editing of your project. You may add text, images, design assets, icons, and

Text: This add in new text & customize your font, opacity, colour and more.

Design assets: This adds additional design assets on your project.

Images: From this, you may access your:

- Libraries
- Patterns
- Photo library
- Files
- Camera
- Free photos
- Adobe Stock
- Lightroom

Icons: This search and inserts pre-designed icons.

Stickers: Browse your GIPHY databank for the animated stickers.

Backgrounds: Look for and insert pre-designed backgrounds.

Videos: Opens your own private video gallery.

Logos: Opens your logo / include new logo from your libraries or your own private photo library.

Viewing and managing your projects

1. From your bottom-right corner, choose Your Projects to see your present and old projects.

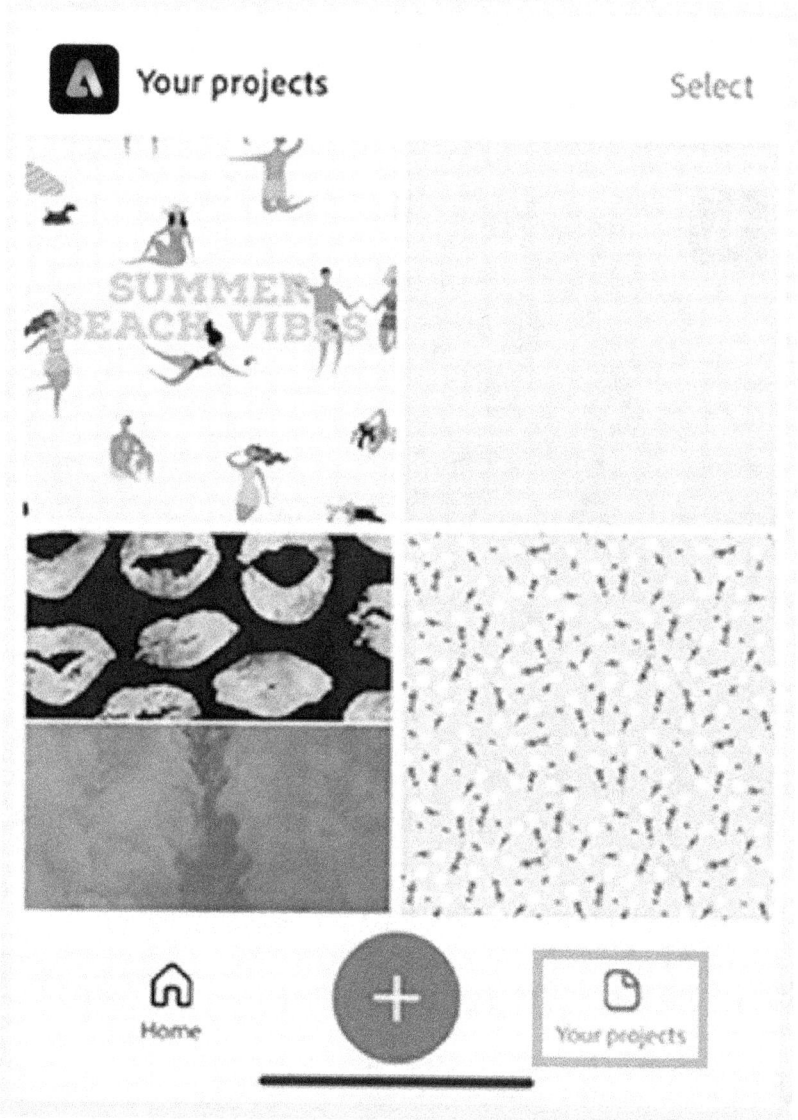

View & manage your projects
2. To choose an specific project, tap on it to launch it.

> On this view, one can edit, duplicate, delete or save project. Select More in order to rename project.

Deleting your projects in mass

1. Tap on **Select** in your top right corner.

Choose your project

2. Choose each thumbnail / project which you would want to delete.

3. Press **Delete** button on your bottom screen.

Sync projects across your platforms

When you would prefer to sync your work throughout many devices with just your Wi-Fi & not with your own mobile data, you may enable this by following through these steps:

1. From your bottom-left corner, tap on your **Home** icon.

2. From your top right corner, press your Settings icon.

3. From your drop-down menu, choose **Sync projects.**

4. Switch to **Sync only over Wi-Fi.**

< Settings **Sync projects**

Sync only over Wi-Fi

Creative Cloud Express automatically syncs projects to your Adobe account so you can start here, and continue creating across all your devices.

DISABLING OF REMIXABLE LINKS IN THE EXPRESS FAQ

You can acquire answers to the commonly ask questions regarding disabled remixable links on Adobe's Express made on iOS.

On 27 of July 2023, the remixable links of the shareable templates in iOS were disabled. Existing files can still be accessed. Original files remain unchanged or can be found. changed. See FAQs, for further information

What's remixable link?

Remixable links are feature in Adobe Express iOS application, where the user may generate any remixable links to shareable templates which are is publicly accessible.

When the shareable template remixable links are disabled, what should I expect?

Previously created remixable links still contain a Remix this design button.

However, as of August 16, 2023, the ability to remix a design is unavailable. The user selecting Remix this design will be brought into Adobe Express, but the template will not open.

My files are not accessible to the person with whom I shared my remixable link. How can I allow them to access?

When you desire to collaborate together with others for just a template, you may send them invite directly to your document. They are going to have access to editing your file & perform any adjustments as collaborators.

On the other hand, when you've got an Express Premium plan / Creative Cloud subscription, you can create template, save it on your library, & share your library to others. Recipients are going to be able to generate from your templates without modifying your original files.

Important:

K12, non-profit users and higher education can generate templates & save them on libraries.

I've shared links to remixable content on public platforms like marketplaces and websites. Now that the remixable links are disabled, what should I do?

Removing any previously shared or posted remixable links will discourage people from attempting to use them.

Can I still access my files?

Yes, you may still view the single-page post that was used to generate your remixable link as a file. The only thing that's gone is the ability to remix your design.

When Adobe Express is updated, will the remixable link capabilities be restored?

We are actively developing new remixable link capability for the Adobe Express upgrade. Stay tuned! As soon as more details are available, we will provide them.

Adobe Express for Android

Discover how you can sign in & use Adobe Express to make your own unique Android designs.

This article will teach you how to create designs in Adobe Express, use its premium and free features to share easily on your social media, and much more.

Sign in

No Adobe Express app for mobile devices? Download your Adobe Express application from your Google Play Store.

Getting started with Adobe Express

1. In your Android mobile device, press your Adobe Express application icon.
2. Log in using your Google, Facebook, Adobe, or Apple ID.
3. You may start creating, importing, editing, and sharing your graphics, pictures, and videos as soon as you sign in.

Getting to know your workspace

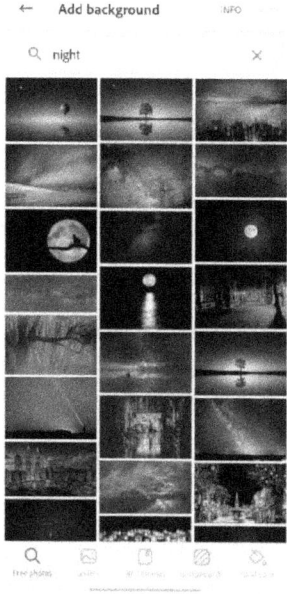

- Free photos
- Gallery
- Libraries
- Backgrounds
- Solid colour

Free photos - Discover free stock pictures inside your Adobe Express

Gallery - Gives access to your own picture gallery.

Libraries: Open your Creative Cloud's library to move assets which have been synchronized on different gadgets to your workspace.

Backgrounds: Look for an already-created background. You have the option to add many backgrounds to your project at once.

Solid colour - Select a solid colour for use as the background.

Create designs and collages

With a few simple steps, you may begin generating your own unique designs.

1. Launch your **Home**. Tap on your ⊕ icon.

9:45
Search all templates
Create a new project
Flyers
Instagram posts
Instagram stories
Logos
YouTube thumbnails
Go premium with a 14-day free trial. Upgrade
Flyers
View all
OPEN HOUSE
JOIN US!
Open House starts at 5 PM.
See you there!
WELCOME TO OUR SCHOOL'S PARENT — TEACHER CONFERENCES
10 Years of Graduates
Instagram posts
View all
ABOUT MY HISPANIC HERITAGE
MY NAME:
MY ETHNICITY:
FAVORITE THING ABOUT BEING HISPANIC:
HOW I'M CELEBRATING:
HAPPY HISPANIC HERITAGE MONTH
Proud to Be: Brazilian!
Home
Your projects

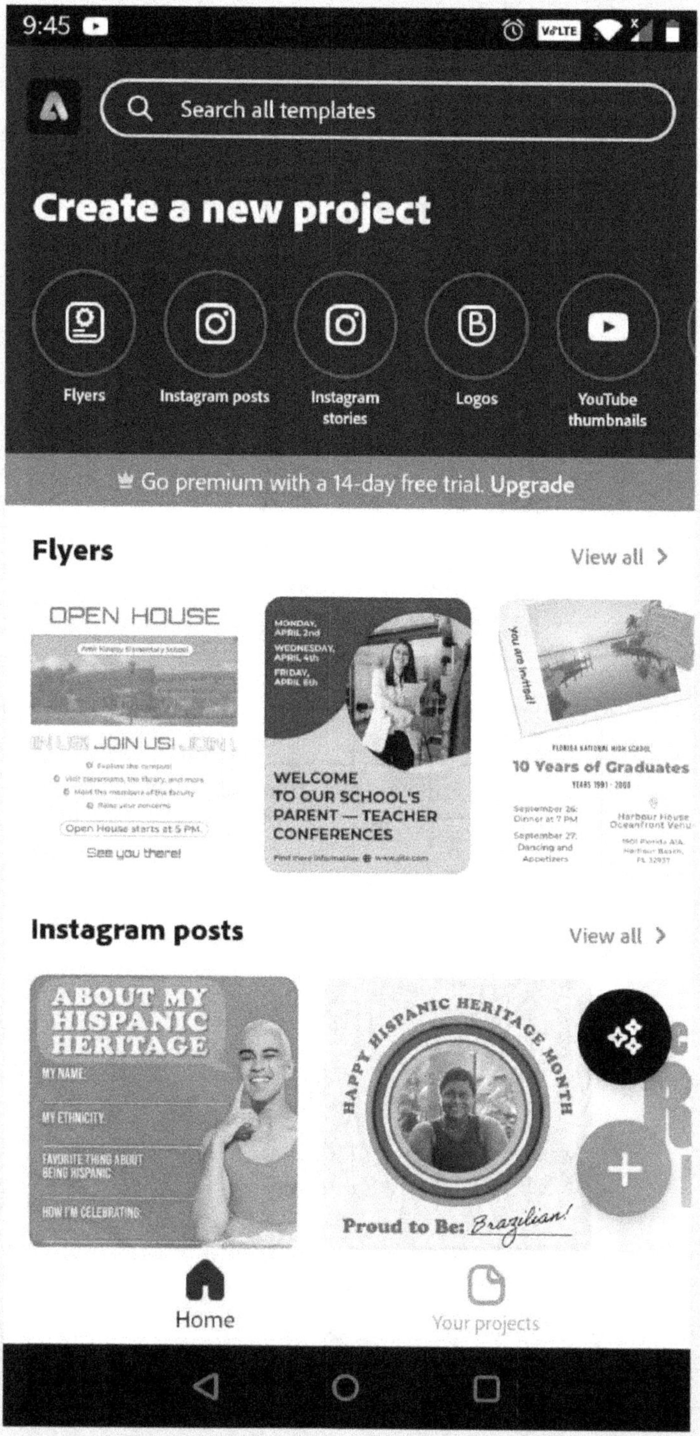

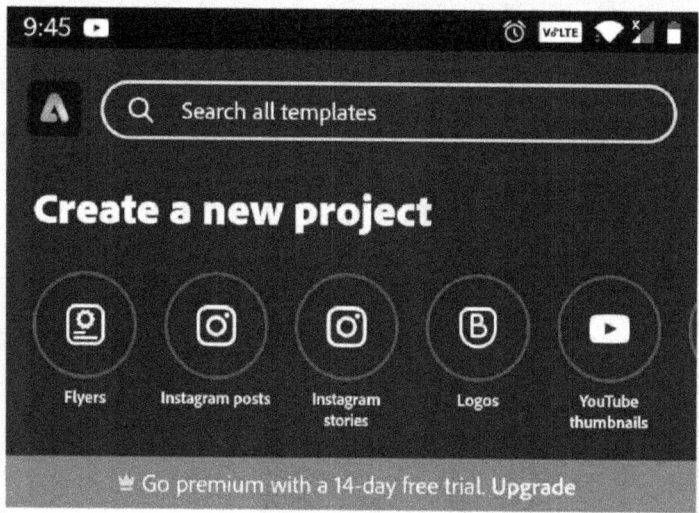

2. Select your desired design option in your workspace option. Click on **Add**.

3. Choose a predetermined size which made fits for your blog **posts, print media, social media**, and other media, or you choose from your custom size to use for your work.

4. Create your project.

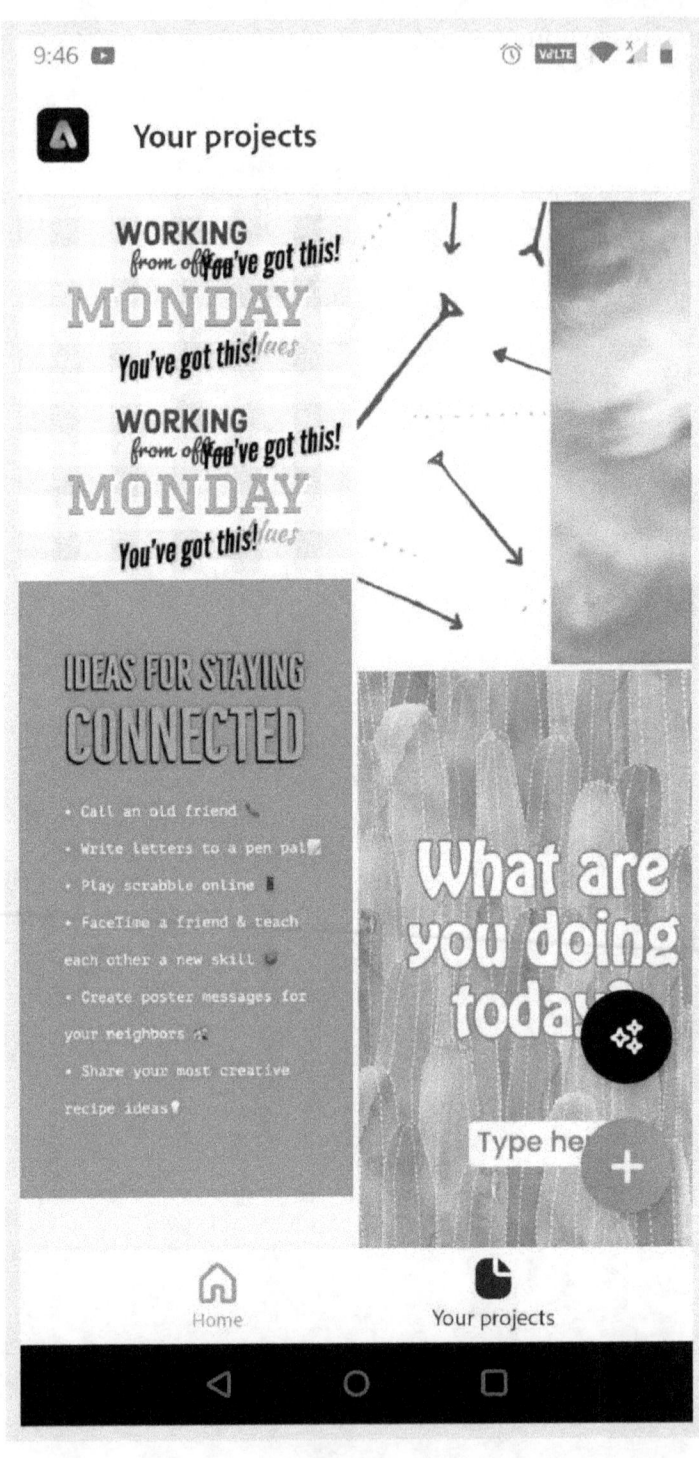

- **Colours** - Helps Select custom colour scheme or pick an app-suggested colour palette.
- **Animation** - This animate your background & your text.
- **Layout** - Choose layout & your border width, collage structure, and explore your pre-selected themes design.
- **Brand** - Swiftly imports your brand assets at just a tap.
- **Resize** - Modify your custom size of your project or choose a separate preselected size selection.

5. Add several pages into your project

- ⊕ **Add** – This makes new pages within your project.
- ⊕ **Duplicate** – This replicate your design on new page.
- **Trash** – This delete pages.

6. Then make edit on your project.

- **Text** - Include new text & alter the opacity, colour, font, and other elements.
- **Design assets** - This add additional design assets to your projects.
- **Images** - From here, you can view your: Lightroom; Libraries; Patterns; Adobe Stock; Files; Camera; Free photos.
- **Icons**: Look for and add already-made icons.
- **Backgrounds**: Check for and include a pre-made background.
- Logos: You can access your current logo or upload a new one from your libraries or your own photo library.

Your Projects

Tap on Your Projects in your lower right corner. Here, you can see both your recent and previous projects.

1. Tap on a certain thumbnail to open your project in its entirety.
2. You may rename your project in this view by pressing the **More** (...) symbol. You can also delete, edit, and duplicate it.
3. You may instantly share your project to your social media using your bottom menu. Alternatively, you could share it with your contacts / a different application of your choice by tapping the **More** (...) symbol.

Your projects

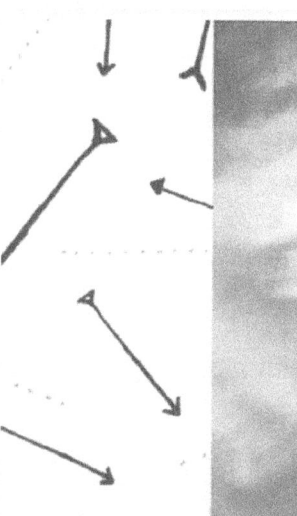

Home

Your projects

Managing Express subscriptions in iOS

Discover how to use your iPhone, iPad, or other iOS gadgets to download, manage, install, & cancel your Adobe's Express subscriptions that you've bought from Apple App Store.

A wide range of iOS devices support Adobe Express.

Downloading and installing Adobe Express on iOS

Adobe Express subscription plan is accessible for anybody for free.

You may download the Adobe Express app from your Apple App store & sign up for the Free plan.

Cancelling your Express subscription

Apple demands that you cancel your Adobe Express subscription via your Apple App Store in your iOS device (or iTunes in your PC) when you purchased it using your Apple device (your iPhone / iPad).

Important:

When you don't possess an Apple device anymore, you can download iTunes in your computer or you contact Apple Customer Support to help cancel all of your subscriptions.

To cancel subscription:
1. Launch your Settings application.
2. Then choose iTunes and App Store.
3. Tap on Apple ID on the top.

4. In your menu, choose views Apple ID.
5. Type in your Apple ID password once prompted.
6. Navigate down then tap Subscriptions.
7. Choose Adobe Express.
8. Then tap Cancel Subscription

Manage Express subscriptions in Android

Find out how you can download, set up, manage, & cancel your Adobe's Express subscriptions that you bought for your Android via Google Play Store.

Adobe Express may be downloaded from Google Play Store and is accessible on many Android mobile devices.

Download & install Adobe Express in Android

You can download the free trial of the Adobe Express.

Cancellation & refund

Unless you unsubscribe, your Google Play Adobe Express subscriptions are automatically renewed. Your subscription will not be cancelled if you uninstall your application.

Google requires you to cancel your subscription via your Google Play Store application on your smartphone or tablet or the Play Store of your computer if you bought it with a device running Android (phone or tablet).

Make sure you are logged into your Google Account associated with your Express subscription before cancelling. If not, kindly switch to your appropriate account; else, your Adobe Express's subscription might not be visible.

For cancellations: Learn more about how to cancel, pause, or change a subscription on Google Play.

For refunds:

- **Cancelling annual subscriptions in 48 hours of initial purchase**: Find out how to request for refund.
- **Cancelling annual subscription after 48 hours of initial purchase**: Get in contact with Adobe Support for a refund or billing requests.

Manage Adobe Express subscriptions on Samsung Galaxy Store

Download and install Adobe Express for Samsung from the Galaxy Store

Adobe Express for Samsung is available for download through the Samsung's Galaxy Store.

Each Samsung devices which support Android version 5.0 Lollipop or higher are capable of running Adobe's Express application for Samsung.

Upgrading into paid Express for subscription of Samsung

1. Tap on your top left menus icon on your Adobe Express.
2. Select **Account**

3. Tap on **Subscribe**. You will be taken to Samsung Galaxy Store at where you can purchase your subscription.

You've already got access to the Adobe's Express when you have a purchased plan already which include it, like the all apps Creative Cloud's membership.

New users of Adobe Express could be qualified for a two-month free trial. Terms & conditions apply.

Cancel your Express subscription

1. Open your Samsung Galaxy Store application.
2. Select **More Options** > then tap **My Page** > then select **Receipts** > then choose Items. Then select Adobe Express.
3. Tap on **Unsubscribe**.

Select the **Unsubscribe** again for confirmation that you would like to cancel.

www.ingramcontent.com/pod-product-compliance
Lightning Source LLC
Chambersburg PA
CBHW050215230526
45470CB00001B/393